Constitution Street

finding hope in an age of anxiety

JEMMA NEVILLE

for my walking companions, HRB and Isobel Neville

Constitutional

1. Relating to an established set of principles governing a state.
'a constitutional amendment'

2. Relating to someone's nature or physical condition.
'a constitutional weakness'
inherent, inbred, intrinsic, innate, structural, fundamental, essential

3. A walk taken regularly to maintain or restore good health.
'she went out for a constitutional'
walk, stroll, saunter, turn, wander, amble, breather, airing, ramble, hike[1]

---

1.   From the *Oxford English Dictionary*, adjective and noun.

A Constitution

———————————— **Amendments** ————————————

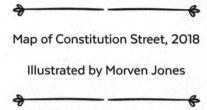

Map of Constitution Street, 2018

Illustrated by Morven Jones

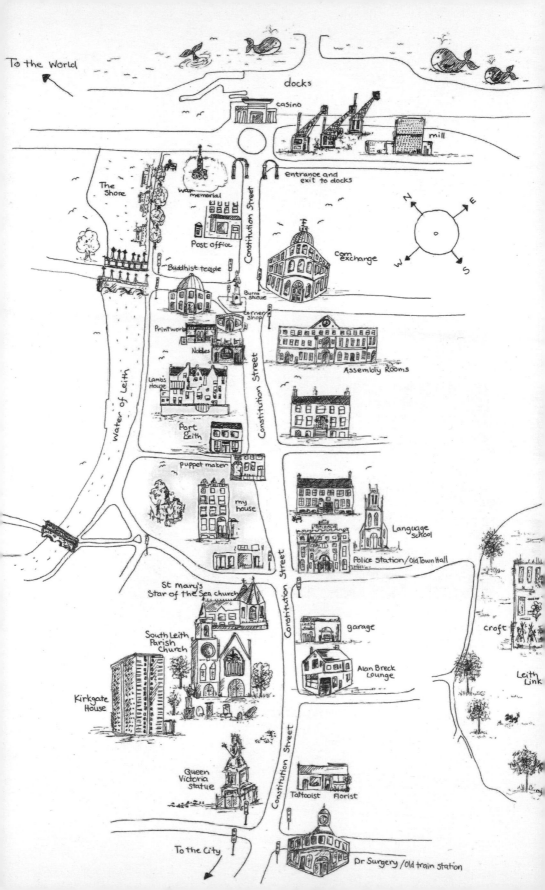

Thou shalt love thy neighbour as thyself.

Leviticus 19:18

Just saying 'love your neighbour' doesn't mean anything, it's just words. Work it through.

Iain, Minister, 140 Constitution Street

Welcome

I crossed over the road to my neighbour's house. The distance from one side of Constitution Street to the other is some twenty paces, if you count them out (which I do), but after a decade of crossing back and forth and weaving in and out between the traffic, it must equate to many miles and a journey well-travelled.

This particular stepping out was in January 2017. The night-time sky dripped black and blue and horizontal drifts of sleet slapped against my cheeks. Earlier that morning, the brass flip-calendar on a shelf in my hallway showed *25/Wednesday/January* when I adjusted the rotating dials, as I do every day, as part of my routine. The black lettering of a new day had somersaulted forward with a satisfying clicking sound into the metallic place-holders. Everything in its right place.

It was Burns Night on Constitution Street in Leith, Scotland, and the year still blinking and bleary. We traditionally mark the annual celebration of the National Bard with a supper of sheep's stomach stuffed with offal and washed down with drams of whisky, usually amongst friends, and strangers who might become friends. Then the performed re-telling of a long Scots poem no one can quite remember one year to the next. Something about a drunken man riding home from the pub one stormy night on his horse and happening upon a witches' dance led by the devil playing bagpipes. All the while, a long-suffering wife waiting at home, nursing her wrath. After the poem, there is a toast to the lassies and a reply. It's a conversation. A song. A quarrel to be soothed. There is union and disunion throughout. It's a semi-autobiographical story of a nation looking inward, which we retell every year.

We have heard a lot of stories in recent years on Constitution Street, and on streets up and down the land, about our differences. The Yes and the No. The Leave and the Remain. The them and the us. With us or against us. The coming and the going of constitutional standpoints and binary positions. Some neighbours put up campaign posters in their windows. Others closed the curtains. Some sang protest songs and wrote poems. Some felt anxious. Some felt excited. I felt a bit of all of these emotions.

My neighbour across the road and I voted differently in the two referendums. By contrast to the multitude of choice and complexity shaped by our life experiences, the referendums presented purely binary choices to voters. 'Should Scotland be an independent country?' Yes or No. 'Should the United Kingdom remain a member of the European Union or leave the European Union?' Remain or Leave. There was no middle ground; no place to capture any measure of the nuances and ambiguities that lie behind a choice of two opposites. Life, of course, isn't like that. It is messy and capricious and all the richer because of it. Many voters were likely a quiet No, a surprise Yes, a hesitant Remain or a protest Leave, along a broad spectrum of preferences and aversions to risk, shaped by personal and public narratives. In one way or another, we are all somewhere in between. Rather, we need to be asking one another, what do we hold in common? Who is my neighbour? How do we want to live together, here, on this street?

Good questions make for better law and policy-making. On 24 January 2017, the day before our Burns Supper on Constitution Street, judges at the UK Supreme Court were asked to consider a significant constitutional question posed by businesswoman and campaigner Gina Miller about the balance of power between the executive and legislature. The court ruled that the UK Government could not remove the country from the European Union without the legislative consent of Parliament. However, the same constitutional law case also held that consent from the devolved legislatures, including the Scottish Parliament, was not required. The constitutional convention of seeking consent in matters concerning devolution had been proved to be just that, a convention and not a law.[1]

A year and a half later, in June 2018, The European Union (Withdrawal) Act would be given royal assent.[2] The intervening months were a time of immense uncertainty for the constitutional futures of both Scotland and the UK. It was an interregnum of sorts while we waited for the balance of powers to settle. The collective mood was one of flux. Anxiety en masse pervaded everything and everyone. Our national identity was at sea, with the rest of the world looking on. Of course, treading water at sea can look like waving to onlookers or drowning alone, depending on your vantage point. One thing we did mostly agree with, on Constitution Street and streets up and down the land, was the need to hold onto our shared values and to try to navigate a way forward in the unchartered waters swelling in and around Brexit.

We needed both a compass and an anchor that would protect our human rights beyond the party politics of the day. The idea of a written constitution drafted for, with and by the people of Scotland had been floating for some time, proposed by legal scholars, but as the UK's constitutional arrangements became more and more choppy in the absence of a post–Brexit plan, the need for a rights framework, in the form of a written constitution, became increasingly real to me.[3]

I was aware that 2018 coincided with twenty years since the establishment of the devolved Scottish Parliament. It was also twenty years since I was a young, idealistic law student marching to make poverty history, protesting the invasion of Iraq and then, in my first job, recording witness testimony and applying international law in the war-crimes courts of former Yugoslavia. The Balkans are a lesson in what can go badly wrong when neighbours stop talking to one another and respect for human rights law is destroyed.

When the law is well-drafted, it unfolds as though on a map. Statutes become route-markers and case law like cairns that indicate changing conditions. Navigating the law as a living document is about observing both the letter and the spirit of the law in the present climate. It is about seeing what is written down and the expression and intent concealed within it.

Human rights law is further guided by principles such as proportionality, to balance individual freedoms with public interest as a whole. The duty of the state and its public bodies to respect, protect and fulfil our human rights, such as the highest attainable standard of healthcare, housing and social security, is about ensuring that we can all live out our lives with human dignity. In this way, the wellbeing and outlook of each of us individually can be seen as a living, breathing indicator of the collective health of the law and of the nation – our combined constitutional strength.

Back when I was a student learning about the law, I took everything to heart in an unjust world. I know now that self-care can be the most useful act of change-making in the world, freeing up energy and compassion to be a happier, lighter person to be around. And of course, most of us are anxious, in our own particular ways of being and doing. Anxiety fizzes in the mind and the belly as we over-analyse past events and worry about the future. It is a self-destructive effort to control the uncontrollable.

For me, anxious behaviour also manifests itself in the most mundane of ways. For example, by obsessing about the placement and contact of things side by side – the edges, the spaces in between, the ellipsis. I might walk as silently and deliberately as possible in between the pavements as though I were wearing moccasins on a forest floor, trying to avoid the cracks. Or sometimes, the anxiety takes the form of willing one hypothetical thing to happen over another, a sort of plea-bargaining with myself. I will challenge myself to reach the next kerb before an approaching bus rounds the corner onto the street, telling myself that this effort will prevent something bad (usually an expected loss) from occurring. The real object of the control and concern is bound up with attachment to people, and the proximity and depth of my relationship to those people. It is with some irony then that these apparently common behavioural traits can be flippantly labelled OCD – obsessive compulsive disorder – when it is the ordering, the attempts at controlling the uncontrollable, that push and pull the undulating waves of anxiety.

But anxiety is not all bad. Hypersensitivity makes us pay attention to detail and subtlety that might otherwise be overlooked or unheard. It engages the empathy muscle. When I walk up and down Constitution Street every day with my dog, Bonnie – our pre-amble – I overhear hopeful stories about neighbours helping one another and of people of different nationalities, ages, faiths, and political outlooks finding common ground. This bears little resemblance to the fear-inducing headlines about division and intolerance in the national and international news.

I started to write down some of the stories, for writing is itself an act of protest against impermanence and uncertainty. It claws at the past and calls out to a future reader. It fixes words in a moment of time. On Constitution Street, I was back in a courtroom of sorts. I was listening, documenting and weighing up testimony. In this gathering of evidence, I sat cross-legged on the floor of my tenement flat and sketched out a map of the street onto large sheets of brown parcel paper and then sticky-taped them to a wall. Over the map, I drew arrows and crisscrossing lines in black pen, showing how the people of the street, my neighbours, come into contact with one another. I wrote down the names I knew and ringed obvious meeting points of connection. The whole thing resembled a crime-scene investigation which I soon had to warn visitors about when they came to my home.

Making the map and then fixing it to the wall of my flat, I was subconsciously marking out the boundaries of my home life and how my attachment to home expands out into the street and city beyond. The arrows and circles that linked people and places became a set of founding provisions for recognising a form of commons with my neighbours.[4] I wanted to know more about the people I passed every day in the street and to be known in return. Who was the person behind a nod, a wave or a smile? What made my neighbours hopeful or anxious? How did they come to live or work on Constitution Street? What did human rights mean to them?

I used these questions to open up face-to-face and side-by-side conversations on the street about how we could shape a future that places human dignity at the centre of our country's law-making. More often than not, neighbours told me that no one had ever asked them these questions before. Unlike in the news coverage of the chaotic months preceding Brexit, most of my interviewees weren't politicians, lawyers or well-known commentators. They were people like you and me.

I also had an inclination that by sending out and receiving these open letters, I might personally feel more grounded during a liminal time in my own life. To be known in the sense of daily recognition – a friendly wave across the street, a nod or smile at the bus stop, or to be offered 'the usual' in a local pub or café – is believed by social psychologists to be a strong indicator of wellbeing.[5] These small, everyday moments of attachment make us feel valued and safe. I hoped that my street conversations would help to make the application of human rights in practice real for me. In this way, I was maintaining, or restoring, my own wellbeing. I was setting out on a constitutional. And, like all of us, I wanted to love and to be loved, by the people I encountered.

You see, I love my neighbours. I don't always like them, mind. Mind, see, ken, like, eh, you know what I mean? Everyday speech is peppered with the desire to be listened to and be known. Conflict arises when we don't feel known or listened to. Ambling up and down Constitution Street as I do each day, my belonging to a place, and its knowing of me in turn, becomes familiar. As fellow human beings passing one another in the street, neighbours are continually observing and amending conventions, codes and precedents for ways of getting along together. Getting here. Getting it right. Like, mind on Burns Night in January 2017?

That night, across the road from my home, I had been invited, along with other women from the street, to celebrate exactly twenty years' sobriety of a neighbour and friend with a Burns Supper. No booze, no meat, no men. For one night at least. Later, when we were gathered inside her house, a vegetarian haggis would be cooked in the microwave and its split insides served with a clapshot of neeps, tatties and tomato ketchup, eaten from plates on trays on knees.

Further along the street at the north-south junction that stretches parallel to the sea, there still stands a commemorative statue of the Bard, Rabbie Burns, dressed in plaid waistcoat and breeches, his right hand raised over his heart. Hidden in plain sight, he hings his head wistfully toward the temptations of the docks, the dancing girls, the honest poverty, the dignities and the hamely fare on which we would be dining at the Burns Supper. For a' that.

Our street is rich too with other constitutional characters from Scottish, British and European history. Robert the Bruce, Henry VIII, Mary

Queen of Scots and Oliver Cromwell all feature. Here is the spot where for centuries Scotland faced the world, as ships set sail from the docks at the port of Leith to the European mainland and wider world beyond. It has always been a meeting point of the old, the new and the in between.

It was at this junction by the Burns statue that my year and a half of conversations about human rights and dignities lay stretched out ahead. From January 2017 to June 2018, I interviewed sixty of my neighbours and the owners of local businesses about our lives together on the street. These sixty people became the drafters of this, a Bill of Rights. We discussed what we wanted to amend and what we wanted to keep. These were our checks and balances for constitutional change. I listened to those who voted differently from me and I challenged my own assumptions and prejudices, to consider what rights, if any, we would want to enshrine in a new written constitution.

Alongside these conversations, the broader context did not stand still. Political events, at home and in the rest of the world, unfolded in unpredictable and messy ways. It was a slippery time for both geopolitics and for me personally, encompassing a snap General Election, prolonged Brexit negotiations, an existential crisis for Scottish nationalism, lessons in popular sovereignty from the Catalan and Kurdish independence campaigns, and opportunities to reconnect with refugee friends as they continued their journeys through Europe. Like a long Scots ballad, there was union and disunion throughout.

My comparative research on constitutional change took me from the Foot of the Walk in Leith, to Aristotelous Square in Greece and Plaça de Catalunya in Spain, meeting with ordinary people living through extraordinary times in their own small places closest to home. Mostly though, I walked up and down Constitution Street every day and I paid attention to change so that I might come to name it, and therefore to know the street, and myself, better.

Welcome

Written in real-time from January 2017 to June 2018, I matched up my diary accounts of the conversations I had with my neighbours with individual human rights. The resulting series of letters to the law tell of hellos and goodbyes, of snow falling and melting, of new babies being born on the street, of politicians shaking hands, of cygnets surviving in the river current and of unexpected and sudden loss. It was the best of times and the worst of times. So it goes in the tale of my city street.

It all started with climbing the eight, slanting slabs of sandstone steps to the house across the road and chapping on my neighbour's front door. I unfurled my scarf and flattened my windswept hair. I shuffled back and forth on her doorstep, to and fro, tapping out a swaying rhythm in heeled boots, trying to keep warm in the soapy sting of January air and to not drop my gift of a haggis. Poised, ready, I hovered on the threshold, on the periphery, somewhere in between. The sky above me and the street below. I knocked again. I pushed open the letter box and called 'It's just me' into the slit of electric light. I watched my breath be absorbed into the gathering warmth of the familiar hallway beyond. I waited. A dog barked. A pair of denimed legs attached to bare feet appeared in the rectangular picture frame of the letter box, hinging and enlarging into view across floorboards like a half-shut knife. My neighbour came to open her door.

Ah, it's yourself, she said. *Away and come in.*

Where, after all, do universal human rights begin?

In small places, close to home — so close and so small that they cannot be seen on any maps of the world. Yet they are the world of the individual person; the neighbourhood he lives in; the school or college he attends; the factory, farm, or office where he works.

Such are the places where every man, woman, and child seeks equal justice, equal opportunity, equal dignity without discrimination. Unless these rights have meaning there, they have little meaning anywhere. Without concerted citizen action to uphold them close to home, we shall look in vain for progress in the larger world.

Eleanor Roosevelt, Chair of the United Nations Commission on Human Rights (drafters of The Universal Declaration of Human Rights, 1948)

Well, we're still talking and that's the best thing. When the talking stops, that's when you've got to be worried.

Donald, Mechanic, 86 Constitution Street

Setting Out on a Constitutional

I was sat at my kitchen table on Constitution Street after polling stations closed on the night of the Scottish independence referendum on 18 September 2014. With me were friends and siblings, people born in different corners of the world but all now at home in Scotland. Yes, No and Don't Know voters alike, but not a flag between us. As we waited for the results to come in on the television, we exchanged memories of the previous two years of debate about national identity. We marvelled at the experience of participating in the most inclusive call to democratic engagement ever witnessed in UK political history – an electoral turnout of 84% and voter registration of 97%. The debate had been overtly Scottish in character – canny, cautious and creative.

News of the pro-Union result was confirmed at about 5am and we began to slowly survey the debris of sleeping bags, empty bottles and false expectations littering my small flat. Some pulled on boots and trudged through the damp, mulching leaves thickening the Water of Leith river path outside. Others busied themselves making pots of tea and scrolling through social media to try to make sense of the new lay of the land.

The morning after the night before, a dense, pervading haar clung to the city. The haar, as we call it in Scotland, is a form of low-lying sea mist. It is a spirit-deflating climatic affliction particular to the north east of the country and, much like a hangover, fugs the mind and dampens the soul. When I eventually stepped outside, I walked to nearby Portobello beach with Bonnie to imprint our footprints and pawprints on the shades of shifting grey sand. When the haar began to lift, I noticed a line of St Andrews crosses pinned to masts along the shoreline and asked a fellow dog-walker if she knew of the significance. *Oh, that must be something to do with those Yes people I should think,* oblivious to the international volleyball tournament we encountered later, further along the beach.

I had been one of those 'Yes people'. For me, voting Yes was a head-over-heart decision. It was a vote for progressive change and internationalism, not any romantic ideal of a Caledonian Spring. I had always considered myself to be British. I lived in London some of my childhood and I feel a strong, cultural connection to all four nations of the UK. However, it was during the two years prior to the referendum that I had my political conscience provoked and I changed my voting intention from No to Yes. At that time, I was working as the Outreach Coordinator at the Scottish Human Rights Commission.[1]

My role at the Commission was to support community groups, such as disability rights campaigners, tenant associations and care home residents to better understand and make use of human rights law. Every day and across the country, I witnessed first-hand the cumulative impact of UK austerity and welfare reform on living conditions – cuts to social security budgets leaving older people isolated, benefits sanctioning penalising disabled people and the dehumanising stigma experienced by people having to rely on food banks. Politics in the UK lurched further to the right, with little or no effective opposition from the centre-left to mitigate the damage. Rather than prioritising the needs of the most vulnerable and marginalised in society, the UK Government wanted to repeal The Human Rights Act and its legal protections against discriminatory treatment.

In Scottish politics, an effective opposition had also been largely absent throughout the dominance of SNP governments at Holyrood. However, the consensus- and cooperation- politics embedded into the Scottish

Parliament's committee structure allowed for cross-party support on issues that mattered to me – the smoking ban, land reform, the scrapping of university tuition fees and coordinated international action on climate justice and human rights. As I saw it, at the time of the Scottish independence referendum in 2014, a commitment to an independent Scotland offered the only real and meaningful opportunity to bolster peaceful internationalism and to take a radically different approach to immigration, defence and social security (all policy areas reserved by the UK Government under devolution arrangements[2]). The population demographics in the UK meant that voters in Scotland, with its much smaller population of 5 million compared to England's 55 million, rarely got an elected government of their choosing.

Many of my family and friends thought differently and by and large we respected our different views and the reasoning behind them. My grandmother, Isobel, made it clear to me that she was firmly against independence. Her experience of wartime evacuation as a child, while Britain fought fascism, made her value union with other UK nations above all else and to inherently distrust any form of nationalism. She couldn't hide her surprise when, during the heady summer of 2014, I told her about my late nights spent making new friends through artists' networks, like *National Collective*, in support of Scottish independence. Sat side by side in armchairs at the window of her West Edinburgh home, Gran and I discussed how in our different voting choices, we both wanted the same thing – the best future for the next generation. However, we couldn't persuade one another to vote differently. In the intervening years, some family and friends have changed their minds and it is of course the right of any of us, myself included, to change our minds again. Self-determination should be a continuum, not a one-off opportunity.

Clearly, the opportunity presented on 18 September 2014 didn't result in a constitutional resettlement. After the result, any *No Thanks* posters displayed in windows on my street and elsewhere were taken down. There was no dancing and singing in the streets. Rather, a sectarian skirmish in George Square, Glasgow, embarrassed the nation and recalled some uncomfortable home truths about prejudice and loss in post-industrial, Central-Belt Scotland. Footage of hard, displaced men clothed in the soft nylon of both Union Jacks and Saltires was broadcast to international onlookers watching Scotland's day in the constitutional spotlight. The whole ghoulish scene resembled the disbanding of an army.

In the aftermath of the vote, media focus shifted back to London. Scotland, my Scotland, felt eerily muted and paused. Paused in the uncertainty of where to go next and fearful of having not understood one another. Most people kept their heads down and battled through the smirry rain of dank, early autumn 2014. The seasons turned as they always do, autumn into winter. A time for lighting fires and starting new conversations.

Excitement and anxiety spark and catch alight at the borders and boundaries of life. Here are the fault-lines for identity and the crossroads to something different. There was more political change to come.

In the months preceding September 2014, many Scots had had their constitutional awareness heightened. Afterward, an independence of spirit and a renewed cultural confidence lay fervent but dormant. Whatever the political future had in store and however we each had voted, it was clear that we would need one another more than ever in the years ahead. Scotland had to become an interdependent nation.

Interdependence was a theme at the *Changin' Scotland* festival in Ullapool, North-West Scotland, in early 2015.[3] I led a workshop where I offered participants three physical states of firewood – timber, ash and kindling – metaphors for the present, past and future. All the participants chose to spend most of the time considering the ash – letting the soft, sooty parti-cles blacken hands and cause plumes of dust clouds. This was despite people admitting to a negative association with ash: 'reminds me of death' or 'I'm always sweeping out fire grates!' The ash represented loss, memorialisation and perhaps also the need for decomposition before new growth.

Next, the kindling was a metaphor for energy and collective action. It is wood with potential that will be committed to the fire. People liked holding the small and light kindling bricks in their hands while they talked together, or quietly assembled small models with the wood.

Then timber. The lichen-covered silver birch and oak rounds symbol-ised roots, knowledge and truth. I like stability and certainty so was most instinctively drawn towards the tangible, solid roots of the wood metaphor.

Ullapool, and gatherings like it, were a time for regrouping as campaign-ers, learning from mistakes made in 2014 and building new alliances out of the ashes of the old. What we did not know then was that things were about to become even more uncertain and anxiety-inducing for the constitutional future of Scotland in the UK and Europe.

At dawn on 24 June 2016, I was back sitting at my kitchen table, alone this time, when I received news of the Brexit vote on my Twitter feed. I was waiting for a taxi to take me to the airport for a red-eye flight ahead of a work-day in London. Another 5am. Another long, unsettling day. And more manoeuvres in the disorientating dance of constitutional change.

One of the reasons it felt like an exhausting, frustrating time was that, in contrast to the debate about Scottish independence, the EU referen-dum in 2016 had, on both sides, felt mean-spirited, lacking in imagination and reactionary. There was no safe space in which to listen to and talk with those who held a different outlook.

The result to leave the European Union highlighted substantial differences in how the four nations of the UK envisaged the future of the country in Europe (62% of Scots and all 32 local authority areas voted to remain within the EU). The months during 2017 and 2018 which led up to the planned departure date of the UK from the European Union were shaped by political uncertainty and economic instability. Negotiations with the European Commission on reaching a Brexit deal floundered, calls for a so-called People's Vote on the terms of the Brexit deal gained momentum and the decision as to whether or not to press for a second Scottish Independence referendum before the 2021 Holyrood elections became an intractable conundrum for Scotland's First Minister. All in all, there was an in-between, messy kind of a feel to the times.

It is of course the arrogance of each successive generation to place themselves as the protagonists in the greatest of historical dramas. And yet by any objective reasoning, those of us born from 1980 onward, known as Generation Y, have come of age in a period of immense flux. It is an age of anxiety characterised by the resurgence of far-right populism across the world, the biggest migration of refugees and asylum seekers since the Second World War, a growing assertion of the right to self-determination by secession regions and the global threat of nuclear war. My grandmother Isobel, entering her ninth decade and old enough to remember the original age of anxiety in the 1930s and '40s, conceded that these are indeed extraordinary times.

It can be comforting then to look up from the flat, digital surfaces of televisions and phones to grasp multidimensional acts of kindness. The hyper-local world view – the view of the neighbourhood, the street, or tenement stair – brings into focus the fact that everyday examples of empathy will outlive the narcissism of party politics. Active, local participation and face-to-face interaction is where we can find meaning in the world around us and define the contribution we choose to make. To do so requires self-expression and clear intent.

Constitutions are formal statements of collective expression and intent. There are many different styles and forms throughout the world and each reflects cultural, historical and linguistic subtleties. They are often born out of a moment of crisis and revolution, such as in Germany, India, Spain and the United States, and can be both bulwarks to change and vanguards for democracy depending on the interplay between legislative, executive and judicial powers. Former colonial territories of the British Empire have nearly all established written constitutions and around sixty countries worldwide have now given constitutional status to the rights contained within The Universal Declaration of Human Rights.

Historically, the UK does not have a written constitution. Our institutions of state originate largely from moments of crisis and revolution in the seventeenth century, before the union of nations that comprise the UK and the development of constitutionalism as we know it now. Ours is the only country in Europe and the Commonwealth that does not have a written constitution. Rather, UK constitution-making is about conventionality – codes, customs and fluid interpretations based on case law.[4]

The referendum on Scottish independence was brought within the veil of UK constitutionalism through The Edinburgh Agreement recognising the principle of self-determination.[5] And in January 2017, the Supreme Court upheld the constitutional convention of Parliamentary consent by requiring the UK Government to get the agreement of the House of Commons on its Brexit deal.[6]

Yet, in the same case, the Supreme Court also held that the convention of Westminster not overriding the devolved parliaments[7] was mere convention and not a constitutional imperative. The UK Parliament did not require the Scottish Parliament to consent to leaving the European Union or to have a say in the redistribution of powers returning from Europe to the UK. The application of constitutional conventions appeared piecemeal and inconsistent. Any residual trust between the devolved nations of the UK following the EU referendum was eroded.

In the absence of a written constitution, there is cause to be particularly concerned about an accountability gap when it comes to the implementation and enforcement of human rights.[8] Significant environmental protections, aspects of employment law, data regulation and much anti-discrimination law will all be lost with leaving the EU.

Considering this threat, a written constitution for the UK has been put forward by academics and civil society but is unlikely to gain any traction in the messy, meanwhile phase of political disorder and the strict doctrine of UK parliamentary sovereignty.[9] However, the Scottish Government, either through current devolution arrangements or in the event of a newly independent country, could seize momentum and legislate for a Bill of Rights or written constitution.[10] Scotland could then invite neighbouring England, Wales and Northern Ireland to join.

When formalising a collective expression of intent, by way of a written constitution, there are many sources of human rights law to draw upon as founding provisions. There are three different levels of human rights law – international, regional and domestic – and these are enforced and monitored in different ways.

Internationally, The Universal Declaration of Human Rights 1948[11] (the UDHR) was written in the bruising, uncertain aftermath of two world wars, the Holocaust and the Great Depression. It was born out of an anxious age, etched by the worst of humanity that persisted as a deep mistrust between nations. As an affirmation of hope over hopelessness, the UDHR recognised the failings of sovereign states to promote and protect human rights within and across national borders at the beginning of the twentieth century. It put individual, inalienable human dignity at the heart of a new world order and proclaimed that all human beings are born free and equal.

In encompassing economic, social and cultural rights, including the right to housing, healthcare and education, as well as the classic civil and political rights favoured by western states, it was a truly revolutionary document, the likes of which it is hard to imagine being agreed in today's fragmented international community. Translated into 370 different languages, it is also the world's most translated document and is rich with poetic sensibility. Indeed, at the first session of the UDHR drafting committee, Dr Charles Malik, the Lebanese delegate, reportedly bemoaned that 'poets, prophets and philosophers' would have been more useful than politicians, diplomats and lawyers.[12]

Our personal narratives are complex too. We possess the power to self-edit and retell different versions of our failures, hopes and dreams to different listeners. My outlook on politics and law is shaped by my experiences and so may be very different to your own, but we will likely still have places and people in common. The 'small places closest to home' that Eleanor Roosevelt spoke of in regards to the UDHR are the construct of all these overlapping and interwoven lived experiences. They are the places navigated to and from, far and away, amidst the ritual and routine of day to day life – the park, the bus stop, the pub, the doorstep and the kitchen table.

The UDHR is a declaration, and as such not legally binding. However it has inspired a range of other international human rights agreements.[13] At the same time that human rights were being developed within the UN system, regional groups of states drafted treaties to protect human rights. This included The European Convention on Human Rights (with a later European Court of Human Rights based in Strasbourg, France), which the UK played a leading role in shaping. At a domestic level, lawyers developed human rights arguments through the common law of custom, precedent and judicial review. Then when The Human Rights Act 1998 came into force, cases under the Convention could be heard directly by courts in the UK.[14]

In Scotland, The Human Rights Act and The Scotland Act 1998 require all legislation from the Scottish Parliament to be human rights compliant.[15] However, less widely recognised is the fact that Schedule 5 of The Scotland Act devolves observing and implementing a full range of international obligations.[16] This includes those human rights agreements entered into by the UK but not fully incorporated into domestic law. On my reading of the devolution settlement, there is nothing to stop the Scottish Government from enhancing existing human rights protections to include economic, social and cultural rights such as the right to adequate food, housing, and healthcare.[17] In other words, Scotland could develop a written, rights-based constitution of its own, either as a devolved or an independent nation, without having to obtain permission from the UK.

Taking all these different sources of law into account, making The Universal Declaration of Human Rights the founding provision for a new Bill of Rights could help us connect the global and the local. Although not legally binding in themselves, the thirty articles of the Declaration have been elaborated on in subsequent international and regional agreements, as well as national constitutions, so as to become largely part of customary international law. Seventy years since first agreed, the Declaration has become a sort of international Magna Carta.[18] As a statement of collective expression and intent, I think it is a good place from which to start considering a new rights-based constitution.

Few human rights, of any source, are absolute, however. They are subject to limitations and derogations, both legal and political in nature. The most sensitive of checks and balances embedded in human rights law is the relationship between the individual and the community.

I think my community on Constitution Street in Edinburgh is special, but it is in fact much like any street up and down the land. It is a place where we get up in the morning and go to school or the office, meet one another in the newsagent, the post office or the pub, walk our dogs and grumble about the rubbish collection. We go about the routine of our daily lives as we always have done. Nothing remarkable in that. And yet, if rights are to be realised anywhere, it must be here on the street.

Much like the interdependence of neighbours living side by side in a street community, human rights are universal, indivisible and interdependent upon one another.[19] Upholding rights is about understanding both our differences and what we have in common. It is about having empathy for one another. And how to develop empathy for the rights of others? You have to think yourself into the story.

One of my favourite storytellers is writer and naturalist Nan Shepherd. She wrote that rather than scaling to the summit peak of her beloved Cairngorm, being in and of the land is the true grace gifted by a living mountain.[20] On Constitution Street, I wanted to find new ways of being in and of my urban valley, a place far from the centres of legal power and the political summits held during the constitutional storm that raged all around. I wanted to navigate the length of the street as one might a mountain or gorge, with tributaries and streams mapped out in the lanes and wynds that cascade downhill to Leith docks and the North Sea beyond. I imagined lingering on the Leith shore and smelling its maritime scents as I stood on the steps of my flat in the middle of Constitution Street with a flask of tea, a rucksack and my dog by my side.

I want you to come with me on this exploration. Take my hand and follow me on the walk up and down the street to discover the people behind the door numbers that will shape a Bill of Rights. It is my hope that you will recognise something of your own street elsewhere in the world and perhaps of yourself too. Hear me to the end of the road.

Leith /'liːθ/; Scottish Gaelic: Lìte, meaning wet, damp

Scots Gaelic Dictionary

We usually talk about the weather. Or mibbe if somebody's not been well, you'll ask after them because you've not seen them in a while, you know. Things like that.

Margaret, Lollipop Lady, 161 Constitution Street

The Lay of the Land

Streets have a beginning, a middle and an end, as stories do. So, by convention, which is after all the constitutional, principled way of doing things, we should start our walk at the beginning. But where to begin? North. Yes, but which north? Some norths are more north than others. It's a bit disorientating at first but all the more interesting because of it.

Imagine a deep, green gorge carved out of ancient sea cliffs made of copper coloured sandstone on the edge of the North Sea. Birds and plants that outlived dinosaurs clung to the rock face, the sides of the damp place they called home. There were thrift pink daisies, pufflings, guillemots, fulmars. It smelt of the tang of sea spray mixed with guano.

This was the landmass that came to be known as Scotland, much, much further down the line. Scotland emerged from under half a kilometre of ice after the end of the last Ice Age about some 1.8 million years ago. As the ice began to thaw, sea levels rose and fell continuously like a sponge expanding and contracting to reveal a shape-shifting, fluid landscape of wet rock, sand dune and moorland where natural boundaries continued to blend in between solid and liquid states for millennia. The shape of a recognisable coastline eventually settled into a comfortable place, its outline more like that from the dabbing of a paint-soaked rag, releasing blotches of blue on green and green on grey, rather than a draftsman's straight line.

Appreciating this fragmented lay of the land and the bigger picture of history and geography is important before returning to the present moment and the task of drafting a new, written constitution for the future. The past is a series of moments strung together. We need to know where we have been – part of the founding provisions – before we can find our way forward.

The point is that a long, long time passed and here we are, right here, right now, today, on Constitution Street where there was once a beach. Look closely at the surrounding street names and you will see clues: Sandport Street, Seafield Road, The Shore. Somewhere at the meeting point of Constitution Street and the Burns statue, there was a beach. A beach with sand and shells and tides and everything. There were so many oyster and razor clam shells that they would have crunched under foot.

Today, we must find our bearings. You are standing with me at the top of Constitution Street, in South Leith (we'll come to that), in Leith (for sure), in Edinburgh (a matter of some historical dispute but present day accuracy), in the United Kingdom (anything is possible), in Europe (for now). We are facing towards the sea and the entrance to the docks with the city at our backs. The river is to our left and the park to our right. The compass dial shows 55° North, -3° West, at an altitude of eleven metres.

Take your time. Turn around and around on the spot like a street dog in a circle and you will see that here on Constitution Street is a perfect place to get the lay of the wider land. Twitch your nose and sniff the air. Lick it. Yeah. It's salty and hoppy and a bit, well, grimy. 'Auld Reekie', they call Edinburgh.

The city of Edinburgh is Leith's bigger neighbour further up the river. The Water of the Leith river meets the North Sea at the far end of Constitution Street. They're pleased to see one another – the river and the sea – as the river has flowed a distance of some twenty-four miles to reach the Forth estuary, all the way from the glens of the Pentlands, through the city of Edinburgh with its many bridges and seven hills, to finally pour fresh water into salt water in Leith. Here, there are over 250 species of wildflower, eleven species of fish and then swans, mallards, coots, cormorants, herons and otters.[1]

The first bridge across the river in Leith was not where the bridges stand today, to your left. The bridge was instead at the shortest point along the Shore, at Coalhill. From the vantage point of this central bridge, Leith was divided into the separate parishes of North Leith and South Leith. So Leith's North and its South were not everyone else's north and south. It has always been an independently-minded place.

This area of Edinburgh that we now know as Leith was once its own independent burgh (1833–1920) and there was a plebiscite, another sort of referendum, on self-determination. Residents voted on whether to remain an independent burgh or to leave and join with the city of Edinburgh. In 1920, Leithers voted by 90% not to amalgamate with Edinburgh but the result was overruled. Memories are long and referendums divisive as more recent times have shown.

Before all of this fairly recent stuff, it's likely that the Roman General Agricola and his troops passed through Leith on their way to Cramond from Inveresk and there may have been a settlement in Leith pre-dating Edinburgh Castle. In the Wars of Scottish Independence, in the late thirteenth and early fourteenth century, Leith was occupied by English troops from 1296 to 1314. Edward II camped in Leith on his way to the Battle of Bannockburn and the original charter giving possession of Leith harbour was renewed by Robert the Bruce in 1329.

Perhaps most significant of all, the Scottish Reformation was signed in the oldest church on Constitution Street. And Leith has been burnt, sacked, raised to the ground and besieged on several occasions by invading armies. It's been fought over by the English, French and Scots alike. That's what happens to strategically positioned, in-between sorts of places. All of this built resilience amongst the people.

Today, Scotland is a nation of towns. Leith's current population of 57,000 makes it a similar size to Dunfermline or Paisley. It looks and behaves like a town and indeed it used to have its own boundary wall and town hall on Constitution Street. Nowadays, the electoral wards of Leith and Leith Walk are said to be the most densely populated part of the UK outside of Hackney Wick in London. Some dispute this fact so it might be some sort of fake news. We can agree, however, that there are lots of new Leithers from across the world at home here.

The population of this de facto town has only once been higher than in the present day, at about 68,000 in the late Victorian era. The British Empire was at its height and port towns were booming with industry. My tenement building, built in this era, is in the middle part of the street, in between the bookends of the Burns and Queen Victoria statues.

Past Burns, at the docks, there is a formal entrance and exit to the street. These stone archways add to the feeling of being somewhere that was once important. The view through the arches was deliberately framed so that ship captains berthed at the docks could align their compass bearings on the straight east-west axis up the street and into Edinburgh city centre.

Look through the entrance arch today and you will still see a picture-framed view of Calton Hill in the distant city centre, with its mock Parthenon, the National Monument to fallen soldiers in the Napoleonic Wars. This is known as "Edinburgh's disgrace" because it has remained unfinished since King George IV laid the foundation stone on his visit to Scotland, and the street, in 1822.

As we stand here together today, the logical thing would be to follow the street numbers in chronological order 1, 2, 3 and so on from the spot marked entrance up to no. 175, towards Edinburgh city centre. That would be logical. But this is not a logical kind of a place. The official street entrance now leads to a patch of overgrown wasteland with a car park, casino, three cranes and a road sign marked, somewhat sarcastically, Ocean Way. Ask someone today to meet you at the top of Constitution Street and you will likely find them at the Foot of Leith Walk, the long street leading uphill into Edinburgh ('Fit o' the Walk' or just 'The Walk'). So the foot is in fact the head of the street body.

Turning to the Foot of Leith Walk itself, five streets converge in a star-shaped formation – Duke Street, Great Junction Street, the Kirkgate, Leith Walk and Constitution Street. At the crux of these, there used to be a drinking fountain supplying fresh water, with five ornamental lamps symbolising the union of streets.[2] Encircling the five streets today, there are three pharmacies, a dentist, a GP surgery, a bookie, a burger van and constant traffic. Sticky Vicky, as some neighbours call the Queen Victoria statue, is adorned in a garland made from the tattered remains of a 2014 Yes flag. Elsewhere in the world, this crossroads might be celebrated as a pedestrian, civic square with markets and trees because, as my neighbour Ritchie sums it up, *everything and everyone comes and goes here*. In this respect, Constitution Street hasn't changed in centuries.

Come back with me now to the late eighteenth century. In 1790, Britain was a mere eighty-three years old. There were people alive who fought at the Battle of Culloden in 1746. Speaking Gaelic and wearing tartan was still banned. Revolution hung in the air and on guillotines across Europe. It was a very constitutional sort of a time.

There were a flurry of Bills on the Rights of Man being drafted left, right and centre. Prime Minister Pitt won an increased majority in the British general election. There was rebellion and sectarian strife in Ireland. Two Quaker delegates petitioned the United States Congress for the abolition of slavery. Flora MacDonald died – a Jacobite from the Hebridean island of South Uist who helped Bonnie Prince Charlie escape the Hanoverian army over the sea to Skye. She later married a man fighting on the side of the British in the American War of Independence. Adam Smith, economist and philosopher of the Scottish Enlightenment who wrote *The Wealth of Nations*, died. Mad King George III was on the throne. Britain was about to go to war against Napoleon's revolutionary France. Robert Burns would die in six years' time, the last years of his life coinciding with a movement for democratic and parliamentary reform that directly involved ordinary Scots in politics for the first time. Burns' eldest child, Elizabeth Park, would be born in Leith one year from the street's own birth. My own ancestor from Leith, Captain James Smith, would be born within a decade – more on him later.

Constitution Street came into being in these highly charged times. In the census of 1791, there were 12,000 people recorded as living in Leith.[3] The new street layout was set out in 1790 at the request of wealthy sea merchants who wanted a broad thoroughfare to connect the port and the city of Edinburgh. The dimensions had to be sufficiently broad for horse-drawn carts to bypass the densely populated slums of old Leith and deliver their cargo of claret from French ships in the docks up to the finest dining rooms in the New Town of Edinburgh. The width of the stone arches above the street's backyards are the surviving clues in the masonry. These proportions account for the prevalence of basement flats and cellars, as the street was built slightly raised up from the older pre-1790 dwellings. Many of the cellars were later used as air-raid shelters and are still connected in a long passageway below street level that could one day be opened up.

The resulting street could have been named an Avenue or Boulevard in 1790 for the proportions are grand and stately. Instead, we have

Constitution Street. Its consonants chew in the mouth. It requires good diction. That's the *how* of the name. And the *why*? That's not as straightforward as I would like it to be for the purposes of setting things in stone, for the writing down of a new constitution.

Naming something is knowing it and defining it. It speaks about acquiring and losing power. There is record of Parliamentary consent being given in 1787 for the creation of a new street in Leith, to be named Constitution Street,[4] and by 1793 in *Williamson's Directory of Edinburgh Place Names*,[5] there are mentions of merchants having their registered addresses on the street. However, there are conflicting historical reports of the origins of the constitution reference. Some suggest it was inspired by Constitution Hill in London, believed to have gotten its name in the seventeenth century from King Charles II's habit of taking constitutional walks there. Yet it cannot be immaterial that the decade preceding 1790 was a moment of constitutional rupture and revolution across the world – most notably, the ratification of The United States Constitution in 1788[6] after The Declaration of Independence in 1776[7], and, across the Channel, the passing of The French Declaration of the Rights of Man and of the Citizen in 1789.[8] [9]

Can all of these constitutional goings on of the time really be mere coincidence to our street story? You will have to make your own mind up. History is, after all, just a series of stories overheard and retold in different voices. Some stories land better than others, and maybe it's all in the way you tell them. This is my Constitution Street. There are Constitution Streets across Scotland, the UK and throughout the world, from Aberdeen to Atlanta and Dundee to Durban. The people who live there will find theirs to be special streets in their own ways. And you probably live on a special street somewhere in the world too. One street that leads onto another – other streets with beginnings, middles and endings.

In realising your rights and freedoms alongside those of your neighbours, you will live together in a social contract. For example, one neighbour's freedom to smoke must be balanced with another's right to be free from smoke. The collective responsibility for organising and paying for common repairs or to clean a shared stairwell can only be enforced if a critical number of neighbours consent. Dog waste, car parking, fly-tipping, noise pollution, cannabis smoke, parties and planning applications, the experience of neighbourhood, on any scale, is a constant balancing of liberalism and communitarianism. In this way, the street is a living constitution. Every street is a Constitution Street. And rights begin in the small places closest to home.

Each of the human rights in the following chapters are explored through real conversations between myself and my neighbours, about our lives together today and about how moments in history have shaped us. Like the articles of a written constitution, the chapters can be read separately or taken together as a Bill of Rights. Twelve different human rights are explored. This is not an exhaustive list of rights, nor have I spoken with all of the residents of my street. Rather, it is a selection of the rights and the stories expressing those rights that I heard.

An Inventory

Saturday, 11am

Distance: 1.6km, 0.99 miles

Direction of travel: East to west from the docks to the foot of the walk

Time estimated by Google Maps: 11 minutes on foot, 4 minutes by car, 3 minutes by bicycle

Time taken when stopping to greet neighbours: 20 minutes

Crossroads: 4

Cafés: 4

Pubs: 6

Trees: 17

Police cars: 5

Bus stops: 4 (2 on each side)

Statues: 2

'No Ball Games Here' signs: 2

Derelict properties: 2

Domes: 2

Trams: 0

Sets of traffic lights: 3

Churches: 4

Churches still functioning as churches: 2

Dock cranes: 3

Car garages: 3

Solicitors offices: 2

Tattoo parlours: 1

Grounds designated as sacred: 1

Memorial benches: 2

Restaurants: 3

Window boxes with flowers: 5

Florists: 1

Public toilets: 0

Graveyards: 1

Languages overheard: 5 (Cantonese, English, Italian, Polish, Urdu)

Neighbours met: 7

Dog-related chats: 3

Fire-engine sirens: 1

Everyone has the right to life, liberty and security of person…

Article 3, The Universal Declaration of Human Rights

At first you just see the tombstones around the church but there's life in that space as well, with people walking back and forth, through and through. And sometimes I see people sitting there, having a drink, feeding the birds.

Temi, Mother, 68 Constitution Street

und behind this wa

s sacred, it has

fo

The Right to Life

Comin Thro' the Grain

It was only after an hour or more spent in the office of John Lawson, Edinburgh City Archaeologist, pouring over detailed digital maps depicting the Siege of Leith fortifications, that I realised we were not alone in the room. I was about to get under the skin of the street.

John's office is reached by climbing a steep and winding staircase inside the Museum of Edinburgh on the city's Royal Mile, past glass cabinets filled with polished artefacts and through creaking, oak timber doors. Within the office, his desk is strewn with lever-arch files, scrolls and hard-back books and is enclosed by a fortress of boxes stacked high in cardboard columns. As I sat opposite John at the other side of his desk, I suddenly realised with a mixture of horror and delight that I was surrounded by the medieval remains of twenty to thirty fellow Constitutional Streeters, in boxes.[1]

The box closest to me was labelled 'Skeleton 880' in thick, black marker pen. Carefully lifting off the lid to reveal the packed contents, John inspected various cellophane sample bags inside containing femurs and fibula as another might enthusiastically explore a picnic hamper of sandwiches packed at home earlier in the day, familiar and yet forgotten about for a while. Most obvious at the centre of the box was the skull. *Oh, a woman!* exclaimed John. He could tell this by the less pronounced brow ridge, vertical forehead and sharp upper margins of the eye orbits.

I cradled the smooth, soil-tinted skull of an adult female in my cupped hands and looked into her sightless sockets.

Most remarkable was the whiteness of 880's remaining teeth, one or two of which had become dislodged and rattled around in the cardboard box like missing pieces from a second-hand jigsaw puzzle. John picked up an incisor and tried inserting it into various vacant slots along her jawline before finding an exact fit. He explained that the absence of refined sugar in the medieval diet accounted for the relatively good condition of her teeth. Yet, in contrast to the sharpness of her pearly-white front teeth, the back molars of 880 woman were noticeably worn-down from a lifetime of grinding grain, the staple diet of the medieval Leither. Indeed, still today, Leith Docks imports large cargos of grain from Canada and the Baltic states – wheat, oats, barley and rye. The mills, including formerly the Grain Silo at the far end of Constitution Street, thresh the different grains to become animal feed, flour for bread and, if the grain is of sufficient quality, some is syphoned off for whisky distillation.

Forensic experts from the Centre for Anatomy and Human Identification at the University of Dundee are painstakingly undertaking craniofacial analysis to reveal the likely faces of several of the fourteenth to seventeenth century Constitution Street-ers unearthed during the six months of excavations in 2009 during preparation for the installation of Edinburgh's tram lines. Some date from as far back as 1315 AD, five years before Robert the Bruce signed Scotland's original constitutional touchstone, The Declaration of Arbroath.[2]

The bodies of nearly 400 men, women and children were found on a previously unknown section of burial ground that crisscrosses the street. There were 302 complete burial sites found and a further 100 individuals in fragments of bones. It is likely that at least 300 additional skeletons were obliterated by utilities maintenance over the preceding decades including in the engineering of a Victorian sewage system and twentieth century telecoms services. Those further pieces of bone were perhaps crunched and ground down into the modern street fabric that we walk upon today. There will be layer upon layer of human story condensed together beneath our feet.

Bone is living human tissue. Earlier in the summer months, while beach-combing in the sand dunes at Uig on the Isle of Lewis, I had found the skull of a herring gull, *larus argentatus*. Grains of sand spilled from the eye sockets, the way time is turned. I kept hold of the bird skull during a week of soli-tary walking and reading in which I twitched like a small bird in my sleep, both embracing and wrestling with isolation on the wild north Atlantic coast. The beak-shaped lattice of collagen and calcium followed me home in my rucksack and now keeps watch on a shelf above my desk.

Although generally acidic, the silty soil under Constitution Street, with its ancient remains of oyster shells, provides good drainage and so the perfect subtle and long-lasting conditions for preserving bone. The archaeological remains are from the ordinary parishioners of South Leith, but, curiously, a third of the bones predate the church's foundation in 1483. As such, some of the burials found may provide evidence of the medieval hospital of St Anthony's, destroyed by invading English troops in the sixteenth century. Before the construction of what is now known as South Leith Parish Church (St Mary's Church pre-Reformation), the hospital chapel appears to have been the place of worship for local trades and craftsmen. We can't know for certain, because the car park of a budget German supermarket now marks the spot.

None of the graves excavated so far on Constitution Street date later than the last episode of bubonic plague in Edinburgh in 1645 when 2,700 people died in Leith – over half the population of the time. In his book *Life and Times of Leith*, historian James Marshall wrote that huge cauldrons for the boiling of infected clothes stood bubbling on the Leith Links sand dunes.[3] The practice of burying victims in mass graves, without coffins, beyond the town walls and the burning of all infected premises may account for this gap in burial remains. So, when the street shape was first laid out in 1790, the Church of Scotland declared that it knew of no human burial sites on the land. Indeed, the gas mains man who first hit human bone digging a utilities trench in 2008 was said to have been somewhat surprised too.

The surprise image staring back at me from John's computer screen was the lifelike representation of a woman who had lain hidden in plain sight for over 600 years and is estimated to have been between thirty and thirty-five, my own age, when she died. Although relatively old for her time, thirty-five can be a liminal age for today's millennial women in the developed world. An age where we want to choose to be both mothers and careerists, or neither, but are constantly reminded by the medical profession and advert profiling that thirty-five marks the edge of the fertility cliff from which we must catch our rapidly depleting and falling eggs before all is lost, one by one, to a cold, barren sea.

The title of J D Salinger's *Catcher in the Rye*,[4] borrows from the Burns song *Comin Thro' the Rye*. Salinger's protagonist, Holden Caulfield, misinterprets the poem in a dream to be 'if a body catch a body' rather than 'if a body meet a body'. In the realms of his dystopian imagination, Holden keeps picturing children playing in a field of rye near the edge of a cliff, and him catching them when they start to fall off, like fatalistic lemmings, one by one.

> *Gin a body meet a body,*
> *Comin thro' the grain;*
> *Gin a body kiss a body,*
> *The thing's a body's ain.*[5]

This body's ain avatar on the screen in front of me showed a blue-eyed, young woman with long, brown hair and a height of 5'1. Her vital statistics read like an online dating profile. I had found a match. Two women sitting face to face across half a millennium of human history in the Leith area of Edinburgh. She was, and I am – we are linked by faint traces of distant mothers and daughters, connected by shared place not genetics, traces now mostly forgotten but every so often, seemingly by chance, re-emerging like a brass etching portrait. Women who laughed, cried, swore, made love, grieved and felt something, briefly, of the messy mix of what it is to embody the right to life.

My medieval Constitution Street woman most likely died at thirty-five from complications in late pregnancy, during childbirth or by catching a fever. The threat from infection was real and ever-present with foreign cargo and crew continuously arriving at the Port, together with poor sanitation and overcrowding in slum housing.

The pixelated woman on the screen in front of me had no name, but she would once have been known. She would have had a family tree; 'all the David Copperfield crap' as Holden Caulfield put it in *Catcher in the Rye*. None of the 400 Constitution Streeters rediscovered from the medieval past have names now, only numbers.

I was sceptical of the sun-tanned, unblemished skin and the appearance of makeup presented by the facial reconstruction in front of us but John explained that this was due to an artist's ink work and that other impressions were plainer and perhaps more realistic. He also assured me that many of the Leith faces brought back to life were in fact a lot plainer, and exhibited shared characteristics – though he wasn't in any way suggesting inbreeding, there were several male and female skulls found with similarly very large foreheads and jaws.

While historians like to tell stories, scientists are in the business of evidential proof. Forensic scientists suggest that strontium and oxygen isotopic analysis from a sample of eighteen of the Constitution Street bodies indicate that around 80% spent their childhoods in the Leith or Edinburgh area, with the remainder growing up within a radius of 20–50km. The vast majority of the population died before they reached the age of thirty-five with peaks of mortality occurring in older children aged seven to twelve. Medieval Constitution Streeters would have been much more in touch with their own mortality than our present day selves.

Someone who is in the business of life and death today is Bill, a florist on Constitution Street. One of the shop's bestsellers is a floral tribute for funeral processions, with names and other words spelled out in capital letters. I watched Bill pin the wired heads of white carnations and lilies into soaked oasis frames bordered by reams of lilac, plastic ribbon. He lined the letters up on the shop counter to spell out BELOVED. The petals appeared like an urgent text message shouting about loss. Bill told me that the flowery letters are particularly popular with local Muslim families and that this causes him no end of strife because Islamic funeral ceremonies are required to take place quickly after a death, leaving Bill little preparation time. *People keep bloody dying!* he sighed.

In the past, bodies were buried on Constitution Street in the Christian tradition of east to west, on their backs in closely arranged rows and only a few inside coffins. For centuries, our ancient neighbours lay perpendicular and witness to the daily tide of street surf washing north to south, up and down, only 1.2 meters above. They were cheek by jowl to the foundations of present day landmarks on the street, places like the florist, Kirkgate House tower block, the Alan Breck Lounge bar and, perhaps most appropriately of all, the Boneyard Tattoo Studio at 177 Constitution Street.

'No appointment necessary, cash only' reads the sign outside the tattoo studio. I knocked and the owner, Ritchie, appeared through the saloon-style swing doors. Despite his best efforts to appear *not really a sunshine kinda guy*, he offered me a warm welcome to the tattoo studio he has run for twenty years on Constitution Street. Stroking his beard and beckoning me to take a seat on the customer couch that has an unpleasant resemblance to a dentist's chair, he joked that, in his opinion, *tattoos are mostly for idiots*.

A self-confessed punk rocker, Ritchie has a particular penchant for tattooing skulls and boasts eighty-six skulls of various sizes adorning his own body. I asked him which tattoos are currently on trend.

You always get your fad tattoos. At the moment a lot of people are going for infinity symbols, like a figure of eight on their side. But this week I've actu-ally been in my element because most customers have been getting skulls, which is what I love doin! So, I've been quite enjoying masel this week.

Tattoo needles punch through the epidermis, the outer layer of skin, and drive ink into the deeper layer that's mottled with nerves and blood vessels. I remember reading that traces from tattoo ink can sometimes be found on remains of a human body long after the decay of surface skin. The body's complex processes that keep our skin free from infection are the same ones that allow ink to live forever below the surface.

As all the graves from recent digs predate the layout of the street in 1790, there are likely to be hundreds, if not thousands, more skeletons resting in a temporal peace further along the street and beneath the wynds and lanes running east toward the Links. Bringing up the bodies has only just begun. Our shifting, liminal land does not lie still.

The archaeological dig in Constitution Street between 2008 and 2009 was one of the largest and most important urban excavations of human remains undertaken in Scotland in recent years. When the contested Edinburgh tram works return to complete the route from the city centre to Leith, former residents of the street will once again turn in their graves when the tarmac is sliced open, trenches cut, utility services dislodged and old bones revealed to new residents under the penetrating light of an expansive, northern sky.

All is often not as it first seems in the city known as Auld Reekie. This is of course a city known for advances in anatomical science and the body-snatchers Burke and Hare. A century before the notorious grave-robbing case, wealthier families in South Leith hired armed watchers to spend nights in the churchyard after a burial, to guard against intrusion. A display cabinet in the porch of South Leith Parish Church on Constitution Street still contains the iron helmet and baton of a watcher.

Leaving John's office in the Museum of Edinburgh, I stepped back outside onto the hum of the Royal Mile to join tourists, politicians and students in the land of the living and memory. Edinburgh, the city of constant dualities, the gothic dark of Old-Town closes and the broad, sweeping terraces of the Georgian New Town, the extinct volcano in a royal park and enlightened advances in science and literature, fur coat and nae knickers – the clichés run down the seven hills. In both its psyche and popular literature, Edinburgh enjoys accentuating the national cari-cature of duelling polarities encapsulated in one entity. It is what poet and Scottish nationalist Hugh MacDiarmid referred to as the Caledonian Antisyzygy.[6] The dialogue of old Edina folk has it too, speaking to one another of *doing away,* being *nae bad* and inviting you to *come away in.* There is constant juxtaposition, tinged with a false modesty.

From John's office, I continued my walk down the Canongate, past the Scottish Parliament, the Palace of Holyrood, Easter Road and eventually back into the belly and guts of Leith. Walking the half-mile length of Constitution Street, I looked up and around to notice the presence of any change on the street. On this occasion, yarn-bombed stockings had been added to the Burns statue and a neighbour in my tenement stair could be seen framed by a lit window. I smiled too at the things that remain ever familiar. A menacing gull hovered overhead with scavenged chips dangling from its beak. As I walked I remembered the stories of how places like the Leith Corn Exchange (now Creative Exchange co-working space), Martin's Bakery (now Pierinos fish and chip shop) and the Grain Silo at the docks (now derelict) all came into being on the street and continue to interlink with one another.

Perhaps after meeting some of my medieval neighbours who lie beneath, I will cast my gaze down from time to time, toward the soil, sand and silt deep below and pat the ground gently with the sole of my foot in acknowledgement of a long line of human connection met comin thro' the grain. For it takes death, particularly the sudden and unexpected death of someone we love, to make us live all the bit more and appreciate the right to life.

We need to keep talking about death as part of the right to life. In death, we are all the same set of human bones and tissue, just as The Universal Declaration of Human Rights reminds us that we are all born into the world free and equal.[7] A constitution must include both the right to choose when to create new life and the right to choose how we want to be cared for at the end. Then when our time is up, we might choose for our bones, tissue and organs to be used to sustain other life or deepen our understanding of it.

People do *keep bloody dying* of course but we also keep choosing to be – choosing life and, on my street, choosing Leith in which to lead full lives. Death teaches us that we all want to be known and commemorated.

On the north wall of the graveyard on Constitution Street, above the wild rosemary bushes in the secret garden, there is a bronze sculpture in the shape of the Water of Leith river path. It was commissioned to commemorate all who are buried in Leith in unmarked graves. The engraved text is from Corinthians 1:15:

When buried, ugly and weak;
When raised beautiful and strong.
When buried, a physical body;
When raised a spiritual body.

Everyone has the right to education...

Article 26, The Universal Declaration of Human Rights

I had a wish to go to school and learn – that I would live in a safe country.

Merwe, Schoolgirl and Refugee

The Right to Education

The Girl Next Door

Sticky-taped to the panes of glass of my neighbours' windows were six pieces of white A4 paper spelling out five words in capital letters and a question mark in a child's deliberate but uneven handwriting: DO YOU WANT TO PLAY? Five syllables, like the first line of a haiku, and a direct, unambiguous question with a choice of two answers. I scrawled my response on one sheet of printer paper, positioned it in my own window and waited for the reply. And so began the first of many surprise conversations during the summer of independence in 2014, visible to all passers-by in the street, confusing Yes/No indy pollsters and reviving the Scottish ballad tradition of etching verse onto street windows.

Maddie is a true child of Constitution Street. On the dressing table in her bedroom, she has the scratched mirror that I salvaged from the ladies' toilets on the closing night of the Port O' Leith bar. The youngest of four, her parents first met in the Port O' Leith and were married in South Leith Parish Church. Like Rod Stewart's youngest child, she was also baptised in the same church. Maddie's father, an Englishman, voted Yes to Scottish independence and is an active member of the local branch of the SNP. Her mother, a Scotswoman, voted No and is fervent in her disdain for Scottish nationalism.

On the occasions when Maddie stays the night at mine and I have to get her up, dressed and breakfasted in time for school, I feel truly useful.

I want people to notice us on the walk to the playground and for some to mistake me for her mother or older sister. These are mornings with purpose.

I wanted her to know that spending time together is not a chore or act of neighbourly goodwill, and so I told her that any time she felt like meeting up, she could simply send me a sign. In the age of instant messaging and emojis, ours became a window-to-window, face-to-face friendship. She has taught me a lot.

Three years on from the first window text messages, we sat on the edge of her bed amongst a detritus of early adolescence and Sunday mornings – teddies, laundry, phone chargers, milkshake cups, makeup samples and our dogs – to discuss Constitution Street. The news in the wider world spoke of Britain's failure to uphold its commitments under the Dubs amendment. The Dubs amendment, known as Section 67, was passed in the UK Parliament in April 2016 amid a campaign to bring 3,000 lone refugee children stuck in camps in mainland Europe to Britain.[1] By the time I interviewed Maddie, the press reported that not a single extra lone child refugee had been brought into the country.[2]

> *Do you want to have a staring contest?* Maddie asked me.
> 'Okay!'
> *Good, but first, fill your mouth full of water. Don't swallow and don't blink!*

I was outsmarted, again.

I wiped away the water and asked Maddie if there was anything that she would like to change about our street.

Well mainly because I've grown up here, I like it because it's home but also because I know mostly everybody who lives here … And it, it can be rough at times [giggles]. But it's nice because it's … you can trust it in a way.

Pink gingham bunting hangs in loops at Maddie's window frame and the bedroom walls are decorated with polaroid snaps of friends in school uniform sticking their tongues out. Being age twelve and in-between primary and secondary school can be an anxious, exciting time. Twelve is the symmetric point on a clock face where ticking hands complete the circle and are poised in a moment of equilibrium, both pointing north. Yet the joined hands do not pause for long, clockwise as they are to continue their rotation, ever forward into new seconds, minutes and hours. Being tall and slender with dark hair cropped at her shoulders, a cartwheeling Maddie resembles clock hands.

I feel terrified! And sad too because I'm the only one going to a different school. I've already made new friends. But they're not really as close as my friends from primary school.

For a school project on the Scottish Parliament, Maddie turned to her friend across the road for help. Her class had gone on a visit to Holyrood earlier in the year and it prompted us to talk about politics and about the Parliament building itself.

'So did you get to go into in the debating chamber?'

Erm yes, but we were not allowed to sit in any of the chairs, which was a shame. But one of the boys in my class, when the tour guide wasn't looking, he quickly sat down — just to be like 'yeah I'm cooler than you!'.

'And did you learn about any differences between the parliaments in Edinburgh and London?'

So I think Westminster is like the main place where they decide what happens for the whole country and the Scottish Parliament is mainly for like Scotland and I think, well, obviously the debating chambers are a lot different too.

'Are you interested in politics?'

I mean, I like there to be a fair way of making decisions and things but I don't think I would like to make a career out of it.

'Do you think that we have a fair country?'

Yes, I think it's run fairly. Though I don't like how sometimes people with more money get treated differently to people with less money. Brexit was not a good decision. Because, well mainly for my mum's job. Like, she only gets paid if people buy things and people are kind of scared to now. So she's not getting paid very well. And also when you go to the airport you're going to have to sign lots of papers and things to go to places like France.

'And what do you think about Scottish independence?'

Hmmm... well, I mean it's quite... I have mixed feelings about it because my dad is very Scottish Nationalist, you know. He is always dragging me to conferences and stuff at the weekends, which is so, so boring. And then my mum wants us all to stay together. And I think that's a good way to think — for everybody to just be together and not separate — because we're less

strong when we're on our own. But also, I don't think we'll be able to go
back into the EU and the only way for us to do that in my head is for Scot-
land to come away and then Scotland to join the EU as a separate country.
But I think that's the only reason why I like the thought of independence.

Distinct from UK elections where the voting age is eighteen, sixteen-year-olds had the right to vote in the Scottish independence referendum. Still several years away from being able to vote in any election, I was impressed by Maddie's maturity in grasping the complexities of constitutional change and weighing up the relative merits of the choices presented.

We matched up the phone pictures Maddie took on the school trip with some notes about devolution and turned it into a slideshow. We were smugly reviewing the efforts of our teamwork when my phone began to buzz with an incoming Facetime call and we paused the interview.

The call was from my friend Merwe, a fourteen-year-old girl from Afghanistan. I met Merwe and her mother, Debe, in Kara Tepe Refugee Camp on the Greek island of Lesvos where I had volunteered the previous summer. Debe and Merwe have since continued their journey onward to Athens, hoping to eventually be granted family reunification status to join Merwe's father in Germany. I keep in touch with the family through instant messaging and calls.

Before the refugee crisis, Lesvos was famous for ouzo, olives, and the Ancient Greek poet Sappho. Reading aloud Sappho's poem *Time of Youth*[3] from my souvenir copy, participants in Kara Tepe's youth group wrote bold, imaginative responses. Stateless, without leave to remain and with the constant possibility of being deported as part of a controversial EU deal with Turkey, young Afghans face an anxious, uncertain future. Merwe's young-adult life has been filled with much rougher streets than the one which Maddie and I call home. From Baghdad to Berlin and

Aleppo to Amsterdam, young refugees are left waiting, spending their time of youth without access to formal education, each day passing much like the one before it.

You don't need to be a legal expert to observe that human rights violations are being committed on a daily basis in Greek camps. There is a lack of formal education for school-aged children, a lack of adequate or accessible housing, and in some cases a lack of access to healthcare. Even in the relatively well-organised Kara Tepe camp, children play next to bulldozers and, immediately outside the camp's exit, children and their parents have to negotiate the walk into town along a busy and poorly-lit highway. Kara Tepe was designed with infrastructure and accommodation for 1,000 individuals. There were 1,500 people when I visited and about 3,000 the following year making the camp heavily congested in accommodating the increase. Over a third of new arrivals were children, and of those, nearly a quarter were unaccompanied minors.[4]

Across Greece, volunteers work independently and in organised groups, filling the gaps left by established agencies. They take over abandoned buildings to ensure people have somewhere to shelter, provide nutritional supplies to young children and establish language programs. None of this can be a substitute for securing safe, permanent homes for refugees, but it is something.

Short-term volunteers, well-meaning grown-ups, come and go in the lives of refugee children, particularly over the summer holiday season on Greek islands. My last day helping at Kara Tepe camp was memorable for me but just like any other day for those waiting in the dust, sweat and frustration, in a limbo not of their own making. Grand farewell gestures aren't appropriate. I said a personal thanks to the young women like Merwe who assisted as translators and welcomed me. Other than that, it was a sincere 'hope to see you soon'.

Late in the evening when the sun had gone down and the camp had quietened, children and some of their parents sat on UNHCR blankets watching Disney's *Peter Pan* subtitled into Farsi and projected onto the walls of a portacabin. Aside from the occasional cry of a baby or the whine of mopeds from the main road outside, there was a settling hush. The kind of collective reverence that makes committed atheists whisper on entering a cathedral or mosque. I tiptoed in sandals across a gravel path toward the camp exit to wait for a taxi back to Mytilene town. As I stood next to a makeshift snack bar and mobile phone charging station, a little boy of about five, whom I didn't recognise, appeared by my side as if from nowhere and tugged on my arm. He called out 'my friend, my friend' in broken English and gestured for me to lean in close. I bent down and smiled at him. And then he slapped me. Hard. Across the face.

I gave him a row and he ran away laughing. But what I wanted to say was, 'Okay, fair enough. I feel ashamed that I'm leaving you here and that you've been ignored. I see you. I hear you. And thanks for the send-off.'

Lost boys and girls marooned in a Neverland of false promises, smugglers and ticking clocks can't fly away and must constantly negotiate the safest boundaries. This is a real land very near to us if we choose to notice.

After the news footage showing thousands of tired, frightened people being washed ashore on holiday beaches in 2015 and 2016 stopped, media attention shifted elsewhere. It became easier for us not to notice that things had got little better for the people left in chaotic camps, nor for the Greek islanders in the communities which absorbed the influx of people and offered charity. When the crisis is now mentioned, the tone of some press and media has shifted from distress for human suffering to a disdain for the 'others' daring to think themselves worthy of a better life in our home countries.

In reality, the disaster of recent years has as much to do with the immigration and defence policies of European countries as it does with events in Afghanistan, Iraq or Syria. Proportionate to other EU countries, the UK has taken a tiny percentage of people seeking asylum in Europe. However, as the popular narrative has shifted and facts become skewed, public sympathy for the causes of the crisis, often linked to the actions of our own governments, has waned. Mainstream media and politicians talk of 'migrants' caught crossing the English Channel rather than human beings rescued at sea. By conflating the separate legal categorisations of 'economic migrant', 'asylum seeker' and 'refugee', a subset of dehumanised person has crept into popular discourse. In not challenging this, we are all somewhat complicit in an eroding of basic human dignity.

It can be hard to know how best to help when confronted with the scale of the crisis. Talking about it is a start. And knowing one individual among the many thousands helps make things real. In a small but meaningful way, it humanises something otherwise distant. At least, that was my experience, and one I have shared with my neighbours at home.

Sitting on the edge of her bed in Constitution Street, Maddie and I waved to my Afghan friend Merwe in Greece through my phone screen. We were then joined by Maddie's mother, Louise. In the heat of a Scottish July day, in the 'Athens of the North', we three women of Constitution Street huddled together under a fleece blanket and could see and hear Merwe and her mother, Debe, inside their new tented home at a camp about 40km beyond the sprawling suburbs of Athens of the South. They complained of sweltering Greek temperatures. Two mothers, two daughters, and me, in conversation.

Through the medium of virtual and digital windows, Merwe and Maddie have come to be linked in my mind. Two highly intelligent, brave young women on the cusp of big life changes. All things being equal and fair, Merwe would be offered a safe, forever home in Scotland, could stay in my spare bedroom and attend Leith Academy. As it stands, Merwe hasn't been to school for five years. The Taliban prevented girls from attending school in her region of Afghanistan and, today, she gets harassed by some of the older Afghan boys at the refugee camp for walking alone without the supervision of a brother or father. She told me that she is avoiding the occasional school lessons offered in Greek for this reason.

Merwe wants to be a doctor when she grows up. *I want to help people,* she told me, *and to make money to send home to Afghanistan.* Maddie wants to be a forensic scientist or a lawyer – she's not yet decided – because she likes watching Nordic crime dramas on TV. Both girls follow YouTube beauty bloggers, straighten their hair with tongs in preparation for a Facetime video call and live with strong, loving single mothers who have welcomed me into their homes.

Maddie told me that her primary school class in Leith had a diverse mix of nationalities and languages, with fellow pupils speaking French, Italian, Polish, Spanish, and Urdu as first languages. Maddie learnt a few words of Spanish in class. Our area of Edinburgh has about 2,500 school pupils and for 15% of them English is not their first language.

A native speaker of Farsi and Pashto, Merwe is self-taught in Arabic, Kurdish, Turkish, Greek, Spanish, English and has a smattering of German. The list of languages are reeled off like flag pins in a spinning globe and hint at the many national borders and the route she crossed on foot and by boat to reach Lesvos. Aged fourteen, she picked up conversational Spanish and English from volunteers working in the Greek refugee camps and is trying to learn German using Google Translate and a dictionary I bought for her. She said it's by far the hardest language so far. If she succeeds in training to become a doctor in Germany, it might yet come to be her most useful language.

I gave her the pocket German dictionary on a return visit to Athens in late summer 2017. When I was a teenager, a dictionary wouldn't have been my first choice of gift, but she seemed delighted.

On his military service, the Greek soldier assigned to watch over our reunion at the camp gates didn't look to be much older than a teenager himself. He gave an apologetic smile from under his khaki cap and offered us cheese sandwiches from his packed lunch. Merwe suggested that we make up our own picnic and head to the nearest beach for a trip away from the camp and soldiers. Debe, her mother, liked this idea too and assembled a tupperware of peaches and a flask of homemade iced coffee.

Theirs is an open camp in the sense that, once registered, residents are free to come and go, as far as limited funds will allow them. Local train journeys are free for refugees and after a short train ride through parched scrubland and a stroll along the boardwalk of an end-of-season seaside resort, the warm, turquoise water of the Aegean Sea lapped at our ankles. It resembled the cover shot of a package holiday brochure and us, the three most unlikely of models, posing as an odd family group.

Debe napped in the shade while Merwe and I prepared to wade into the sea for a swim. Not planning for a day at the beach, I hadn't brought a costume and, instead, was sweating under long sleeves and a scarf. I had tried hard – too hard, perhaps – not to offend my Muslim hosts and looked and felt a bit ridiculous fully clothed in the midday Greek sun. I opted to roll my trouser legs up to the knees and strip to a vest. Merwe, meanwhile, had removed her hijab and ran confidently into the waves wearing her light summer dress and leggings. Turning around to see what was taking me so long, she shook her head in dismay and shouted back to me, loud enough for all on the beach to hear and understand, *Jemmy! You're European – take some clothes off!*

I thought back to my own primary school experience, writhing and twisting on a wooden gym bench, learning through doing how to skilfully remove thick, red woollen tights and starched cotton pinafore without revealing an inch of white flesh to my classmates or teacher. These were the elaborate moves of a practised circus artist or a Scottish school pupil changing for PE.

I looked around at the bronzed Greek goddesses sunbathing topless under parasols on the shoreline with their young children building sand-castles, all happily naked. Everyone was now staring at the multicultural, intersectional spectacle unfolding in the waves. I quickly peeled to my mismatched bra and pants and stomped, laughing and squealing, into the salty sting of the old Aegean with my new friend.

Our limbs fully submerged by water and only our heads and shoulders bobbing above the surface, we became two women dancing, playing and, at home, in our own bodies. Fluid and free. Powerful and equal. Bathed in the joy of summer. Brown skin and white skin tones refracted by the blinding midday light to become a continuous marbling of human shapes thrashing in the sea – happy and safe in the sensation of being able to still touch the seafloor with our feet. Debe waved from the shore. Merwe somersaulted like a mermaid gymnast. I attempted to copy but made wide, sweeping circles with my arms underwater instead. We said nothing but splashed and grinned and were carefree for a few stretchy minutes.

'How did you learn to swim so well?' I gasped, carelessly, regretting the words as soon as I had spoken them. Merwe pretended not to hear and held her breath underwater. The bond had been broken and we were back to being heavy and anchored in our established roles. We put our feet back down onto the seafloor.

Afghanistan is a landlocked country. To reach Europe's border by foot is a perilous journey fraught with danger across the Hindu Kush mountains bordering Pakistan, then on into the vast expanse of politically volatile

Iran and Turkey, all the while relying on intelligence from further up the line, from those who have made the journey before, as to where to avoid Taliban strongholds, Daesh terrorism, Middle Eastern proxy wars and military checkpoints. No one chooses to leave their homeland and extended family without very good reason. These are people who have experienced considerable trauma. Mothers and daughters like Debe and Merwe fled in the middle of the night with only the clothes on their backs and a sense of self-belief.

The crossing from Turkey to Lesvos in Greece is five miles at its short-est point and looks about the same width as the Firth or Forth between Edinburgh to Fife, but it is anything but straightforward when crossed in the dark with poorly equipped boats and no sailing experience. It has been a migration route in both directions for centuries and was a hotspot for people escaping violence and persecution at the height of the recent refugee crisis. Refugees arrived in inflatable dinghies, often with poor or faulty life jackets supplied by people-smugglers.

On the night that they first tried to cross the Mediterranean Sea, Merwe's family, and the others travelling with them, were instructed to travel on separate boats – one for men, one for women. The boat with the men made it to Lesvos safely but the women's boat was stopped by a border patrol boat and returned to Turkey. Merwe and Debe suddenly found themselves on a different continent from Merwe's father. The family were able to keep in contact through social media on mobile phones so the women knew that Merwe's father had made it to Germany. However, it was a further two years before Debe had saved up enough money from sewing jobs in Turkey to be able to attempt the crossing once more.

In this same sea where Merwe had previously spent a long, dark night treading water and clinging to the side of an upturned dinghy before being rescued by a Frontex ship, we felt our holiday skin begin to wrinkle uncomfortably with salt and we paddled back to the shallows to dry in the afternoon sun. We ate slices of peach with Debe and dozed for the rest of the afternoon until it was time to catch the last train home. Me on one side of the tracks and my friends on the other. We headed home to a refugee camp and a guest house in Athens respectively – temporal, transient homes.

So, see you in Germany or Scotland one day soon! Inshallah! they called out. Waiting at the train station, a crimson, angry sky beat down on the cluster of faded waterfront hotels, the setting sun casting long splinters of shadow onto the train tracks in front of us and marking the turning of another day. This time the waiting had been a nice waiting, a different kind of waiting. I noticed Merwe's mother sharpen a twig against the metal arm of a bench on the platform and then scratch lines into the pale, honey-coloured hues of an olive tree trunk. It reminded me of a teenage girl graffitiing her school desk or jotter with an inky biro. The date 14/04/14 emerged inside a heart-shaped bubble. This is the date when the family left their home in Afghanistan. It is a date forever etched in their minds. It signifies where the women are from and where they want to return, with their grandchildren and great-grandchildren one day.

In this strong sense of cultural identity, they have much in common with the thousands who travelled across Europe in search of a safe place to call home seventy years ago, at the time that The Universal Declaration of Human Rights was drafted. They are exactly the sort of people we should want to welcome as new neighbours. New Scots must be valued contributors to any new, written constitution. A constitution that is fit for purpose will not leave anyone behind in the journey of shaping and amending it.

On my journey home from Greece, I thought back to what Maddie and I were doing in spring 2014 on Constitution Street. On 8 March,

International Women's Day, Maddie's mother, had asked if I could pick Maddie up from gymnastics class after school and babysit while she worked late. After collecting Maddie from her cartwheeling, I asked her if she wanted to come with me to a spoken word event at the Scottish Storytelling Centre on the topic of gender and power. To my surprise, she was keen. We enthusiastically listened and clapped in response to a series of personal narratives about the fourth wave of feminism, all delivered by confident, young women. I relaxed into my theatre seat and felt a self-congratulatory glow, pleased to be educating my young friend on the ways of the sisterhood. Then the final act of the night. A performance piece about women's empowerment and the reclaiming of body language – every stanza concluding with a rallying call for liberation from the patriarchy and a prompt for the audience to call out in unison an increasingly loud, resoundingly clear shout of 'CUNT!' I winced, slunk into my seat and pulled up the furry hood of my young neighbour's puffa jacket over her head.

Travelling home in my car afterward, through the cloaked dark of old Edinburgh to Leith, I turned down the car stereo, 'So, there were some strong words at the theatre tonight, Mads. Should we have a chat about that, together with your mum maybe?' *Jemma,* she sighed, deadpan, look-ing straight ahead. *When were you last in a school playground?*

Not for the first time, this clever, curious girl next door had something to teach me. They say it takes an entire village to raise a child, but a street is a good place to start.

Everyone has the right to a standard of living adequate for the health and well-being of himself and of his family, including food, clothing, housing and medical care and necessary social services, and the right to security in the event of unemployment, sickness, disability, widowhood, old age or other lack of live-lihood in circumstances beyond his control…

Article 25, The Universal Declaration of Human Rights

You need a warm, safe home you can be secure in.

Gordon, Labour Councillor for Leith

The Right to Housing

Our House, in Our Street

1982. Argentine soldiers landed on South Georgia Island (also known as Port Leith after the whaling station established by Christian Salvesen Ltd.) precipitating the Falklands War. Canada repatriated its constitution to gain full political independence from the UK. Unemployment in the UK reached its highest levels since the depression of the 1930s. Half a million council houses were sold off under the right to buy scheme, and a ska band called Madness released their chart hit single, *Our House*. It was a significant year for many reasons. It also happened to be the year I was born. My inventive parents made their firstborn child a time capsule containing a copy of *The Dundee Courier*, a Rubik's Cube, *Good Housekeeping* magazine, souvenir coins marking the birth of Prince William and the *Our House* record.

On Constitution Street, in 1982, the Pierino family were preparing to open their first fish and chip shop, Mary was negotiating the lease on the Port O' Leith pub, the first batch of heroin arrived into Leith and the late-Victorian tenements in the middle of the street were condemned for demolition by Edinburgh City Council. The fact that the building that is now my home was saved from the bulldozer is testament to the steely determination of its last social-housing tenant, who refused to be moved. I haven't been able to trace this remarkable woman but Mary remembers seeing a large skip on the street filled with coin-operated electric meters ripped out from the inside of the flats:

So you see, that's a wee story inside another wee story. I'm sure they condemned it whole. But there was one woman stayed there and wouldn't leave so they couldnae...By the time that they actually managed to move her, everything was becoming you know, what would you call it...sort of upmarket.

Eventually, the Council relented and the building that had stood witness to 200 years of change was repaired rather than replaced. There are now fourteen privately owned flats within my 'sort of upmarket' tenement. All are occupied by one or two people. My flat was the last to be renovated and to have an indoor toilet installed. However, the flat's thistle and rose cornicing is original and is repeated inside the old print works at number 42, now converted into a café, a building I would come to know well after a decade of visits to buy stationery and then cappuccinos.

The indents in the stone steps that connect each flat in the stairway hint at the weight of the lives that have worn them smooth. Like the inside of a mortar bowl, they have been softened by the constant grinding of many, many feet. And perhaps too the occasional Christmas tree, or piano, being heaved up and down. I think about the measure of these lives past and present while I sit on my stoop outside the main front door, watching the world go by with my ageing dog, Bonnie. Like me, she was looking for her own safe home in the summer of 2008.

We can learn so much from dogs, including their ability to transition from one place to another by shaking their entire body as if pressing reset.[1] Dogs also yawn when they are anxious, as Bonnie did when I first met her as a scared pup in the rescue shelter. She still yawns occasionally as, also like me, anxiety is part of her temperament. Mostly though, she wags her tail happily on our daily walks up and down the street. She instinctively knows how to breathe long, calming exhales and she lets me lay my head on her warm, velveteen belly as it rises and falls. As everyone with a rescue dog knows, she found me. Adopting this skinny, black terrier from the Edinburgh Dog and Cat Home was the best decision I have ever made, closely followed by setting up home in a tenement flat on Constitution Street.

There is a Scottish expression favoured by older women in tenements, 'whits fir ye willnae pass ye by', meaning that everything happens for a reason. Like most of the other current owners in the stair, I was a first-time buyer. In the naivety and excitement of home ownership, I spent about as much time looking around the flat as I would now take trying on a pair of shoes. I had never heard of Constitution Street before. I barely knew Leith. The main front door didn't shut properly (it still doesn't), the stairwell smelt of cannabis (it still does) and there were mice droppings in all the kitchen cupboards. The Woolworths at the end of the street – such a recognisable emblem of a 1980s childhood – was already boarded up as the first casualty on the street of the 2008 global economic crash. None of this passed me by.

My new home had solid, stone walls, light flooding through the cracks in the wooden shutters each morning and floor-to-ceiling windows onto a street scene that I would never tire of gazing upon. In August 2008, I unrolled my sleeping bag onto the bare, splintered floorboards of my empty bedroom and stayed awake all night, listening to the creaks and groans of a 200-year-old story I was hearing aloud for the first time. Some days later, my dad and brother arrived with a hired van full of old, and heavy, family furniture. Dad negotiated the help of two strong regulars in the Port O' Leith pub to drag an antique wardrobe up the worn steps of the stair. I had officially moved in and was making my own marks on the building.

I thought I would stay about two years only and yet here I still am, unexpectedly. Our homes are more than stone walls and pretty shutters. The people who live, laugh and linger a while make a house become a home and memories of past homes are part of what we take with us and unpack somewhere new.

Labour councillor Gordon Munro recalled his first family home next to Constitution Street:

> *The house is gone now. It was condemned really because it was slum hous-*
> *ing – communal toilet on the landing, drying green on the roof. There's*
> *actually a picture of me running about as my mum's got the drying on the*
> *roof. So when we moved to brand new council housing across the city, there*
> *were luxuries like an indoor toilet, you know. A lot of people from Leith*
> *that happened to. There was quite an emigration from the early 1960s*
> *through to the mid '70s because housing was just inadequate.*

Rather than repair inadequate housing, the local authority policy at the time of Gordon's childhood was to remove and relocate families who, in some instances, had lived four or five generations within the same post-code. Today, Edinburgh's population is half a million and three quarters of households are occupied by two or fewer people.[2] Constitution Street is relatively unusual in retaining a mix of commercial and residential prop-erties, including sheltered housing from the 1980s, Georgian merchant houses which are now solicitor offices, Victorian tenements like mine and a 1960s tower block.

A quick search of the street on property letting site Airbnb shows up 236 rooms for short-term rent on the street and its tributary lanes and wynds, ranging in price from £20 a night for a single room mid-week to £400 a night for a large house over the August festival season or Hogmanay celebrations. Descriptions include 'cosy', 'elegant', 'quirky' and 'whisky penthouse'. The short-term, holiday rental market has become saturated, exacerbating existing pressure on available housing. According to some, the concentration of Airbnb listings in Edinburgh is four times higher than that in London or Paris, with Leith being at the heart of this boom.[3] At times, it feels like my street is under siege from property developers, where historically it had been under siege from feuding monarchs and religions factions.

Often associated with the gentrification of urban living today, high-cost letting is nothing new. In the fifteenth century, King James IV owned the Water of Leith river and its harbour. He granted Edinburgh trades-men – the burgess – rights to all maritime custom in Leith, resulting in centuries of strife between the people of Edinburgh and Leith. Taxes were administered in Burgess Street, a tributary in between the Shore and Constitution Street, where Lamb's House still stands.

Built around 1610, Lamb's House is best known for being on the site where the Lamb family are reputed to have entertained Mary Queen of Scots on her arrival in Leith on 19 August 1561. Arriving from France earlier than scheduled, court staff at Edinburgh Castle were not ready to welcome her. Queen Mary stepped off the quayside at Leith docks to a cold, August haar and an even chillier reception from her subjects in the newly reformed Protestant Scotland. *In the end is my beginning* said Mary famously of her later, captive, life.

Lamb's House is now home to Icelandic Consular, Kristin Hannesdot-tir. On a first date, her husband, a fellow architect, took Kristin on a drive to see Lamb's House in Leith. Kristin explained:

> *For an architect, it might be the most interesting house in Edinburgh. If you*
> *look at the detail in the windows for example, you can see where Charles*

Rennie Mackintosh drew inspiration. And it's one of the few buildings of its age still intact. There were sixteen booths on the ground floor — the big openings were like shops and the common stair was open to the elements. Each floor contained separate flats with their own fireplaces. So these were the original serviced apartments of Edinburgh.

The husband and wife team now head up one of the country's most respected conservation architecture practices. Restoring Lamb's House to its former glory has been a labour of love, with hand-forged iron work installed in the windows and larch timber boards used in the floors and ceilings. Here is a twenty-first century conservation of a seventeenth century serviced apartment block, adapted from a sixteenth century townhouse or palace. It's *a wee story within a wee story* that reveals something of changes to housing in Edinburgh as a whole.

The density of urban living in the old town once brought all social classes into collision and conversation with one another. Merchants lived on the highest levels of tenements, the upper classes were resident in spacious flats in the middle and those whom writer Robert Louis Stevenson described as 'the grand men of war'[4] were at home in the closes and cellars beneath. Unlike the symmetrical squares in the carefully planned grid of New Town Edinburgh, people of all walks of life came into contact with one another on the Old Town streets.

The same was true of the molten mix of different housing styles in old Leith. The densely populated slum housing, together with the tanning pits and soap factories along the riverbank, were within sniffing distance of palatial dwellings like Lamb's House and the merchant mansions on Constitution Street where many local people were employed as domestic servants. The cumulative lack of any town planning in Leith over centuries has resulted in the tangle of residential and commercial styles that is now part of the charm that property developers are cashing in on.

The area currently has the lowest rate of owner-occupation (53%) and also the highest rate of tenement properties (75%) in the city.[5] If lucky, we get to choose where we live and who we live with but we don't typically get to choose whom we live next door to. Tenement living locates perfect strangers in an intimate proximity to one another. Our domestic lives are boxed and stacked one on top of the other in a precarious human tower. Our noses tell us what our above and below neighbours cook for their tea, our ears are alert to the quarrelling and the making up in bedrooms and our eyes see what is being delivered in the post.

We know more about our neighbours than we do many of our own relations. This is as much true in Edinburgh as in any city. In her water-colour painting 'Windows in the West', Glasgow artist, Avril Paton, depicts the external profile of a Glasgow tenement on a snowy winter's eve. Inside, the neighbours are continuing their intimate lives, seemingly oblivious to one another and yet side by side and seen by the artist, and us the viewer, they live in one single composition. A man sits at a computer, another draws open curtains to watch the falling snow, a cat sits on a window ledge and Paton includes herself standing at the front door of the four-storey building. We see one another. And so, we see ourselves, in the collective experience of housing.

Our right to housing is also an enabler to other human rights, including health and education. Chief Executive of the Port of Leith Housing Association (POLHA), Keith Anderson, told me that the housing association was established in 1975 by the Rector of Leith Academy in response to there being 'too many children with no space at home to study'. Nearly fifty years ago, teachers knew that poor quality housing affects educational attainment. Today, POLHA has its office on Constitution Street in a striking building fronted by brightly coloured squares resembling a

Mondrian painting. Opposite at number 133–135 is the only housing stock on Constitution Street still owned by the housing association. Until recently, this was sheltered housing constructed to fill a vacant brownfield site, a gap caused by a fire that ravaged an entire section of the street.

In January 1978, a warehouse and whisky bond burst into flames and hundreds of the street's homes and businesses had to be evacuated as fire took hold. Firefighters were several weeks into a UK-wide strike over pay during that winter of discontent, so it was the army who tackled the blaze. Grainy, colour photographs taken at the time appear as though in monochrome. The charred stonework contrasts with the slush of old snow. A soot-stained slither of the former warehouse building still stands as a reminder of this inferno and the need for safe housing.

Soon, the 1980s flats that replaced the warehouse will be sold off for student accommodation, mirroring a trend taking place across the city for single-use, high-cost housing that risks disrupting the diversity of housing stock and therefore the diversity of the people who call the street home. In planning law in Scotland, there is no right of appeal for communities that object to plans, in the same way there is for developers. Many of my neighbours told me they are worried our city streets will soon become homogeneous investment portfolios rather than a mix of affordable homes.

Diversity, the tapestry of a mixed community, was the social justice dream envisaged by architect of the National Health Service, Nye Bevan, when health and housing were a combined ministerial portfolio in 1948.[6] Keith Anderson from POLHA explained to me that the Leith housing association has a policy of combining social and mixed rent housing and of never branding properties so that the distinction isn't visible. There are an average of 240 bids for every single property advertised, highlighting both the scale of the demand as well as the limited supply. 40% of tenancies are allocated to people who are homeless and the most common demographic of tenants is single parents with two children.

The Homelessness etc. (Scotland) Act 2003 is regarded to be world-leading legislation in that it takes a rights-based approach to homelessness, rather than assessing needs by 'deserving or undeserving'.[7] It was intended to ensure that anyone presenting as unintentionally homeless can enforce a right to settled accommodation. However, intentionality is a very tricky thing to assess. Relationship breakdowns, unemployment, mental and physical ill-health, addiction issues and poor life choices are the realities that don't fit so neatly into tick-box assessment sheets.[8]

In the winter months, I met Mark outside the corner shop on Constitution Street. He was sitting on the snow-covered ground inside a thin sleeping bag and begging for spare change from passers-by. As a young, single man without children, he isn't deemed a priority for social housing allocation by the local authority. Constitution Street and the surrounding streets have been his home, on and off, for the last ten years. He told me that it wasn't always this way but that a combination of alcohol addiction, family breakdown and bad luck have left him with no option other than to take to the streets.

In the severest of winter weather, several church halls across the city have issued an open call to those in need of a warm, dry space during the freeze but Mark explained that he tries to avoid the larger shelters because of the risk of alcohol-related problems when coming into contact with other rough sleepers. Some days are better than others, Mark said, and he can scrape together the £22 needed for a night in a bed and breakfast hostel. Other times he isn't so lucky: he has had buckets of water thrown over him and has been kicked out of the relative warmth of a tenement stairwell. Mark's right to housing is clearly being routinely breached by having to sleep rough.

Homelessness is never the whole story. It is both a symptom and a cause of other rights violations. Despite the local authority having a policy to not house children in temporary bed and breakfasts for more than one week, there is often no other option due to the lack of available housing stock.[9]

Under UK welfare reform, social housing tenants deemed to have more bedrooms than they require have their housing benefit reduced. The United Nations Special Rapporteur on adequate housing, Raquel Rolnik, visited Edinburgh as part of a research mission in 2013.[10] Commenting on her findings, Rolnik called for the bedroom tax policy to be suspended because it 'negatively impacts on the right to adequate housing and general well-being of many vulnerable individuals and households'. Her report noted that lack of investment in housing over several decades meant that the UK faced a crisis of housing affordability and availability: 'The right to housing is not about a roof anywhere, at any cost, without social ties.'

Home is about the right to live somewhere in security, safety and dignity.[11] Violations of the right to housing can kill. The Grenfell Tower tragedy in the summer of 2017 was a shock wake-up call about the persistent class and racial inequalities across the UK. That a failure to safely maintain public housing stock could result in the deaths of seventy-two people, many of them refugees or from immigrant families, in one of London's wealthiest boroughs, prompted David Lammy MP to describe London as a modern-day tale of two cities. The need for radical housing reform was urgent.

On Constitution Street, Kirkgate House is a high-rise tower of seventeen floors. I went to visit JP, a neighbour who lives on the sixteenth floor, two months after the Grenfell fire. It was also the first day of the Edinburgh Festival. A theatre director and avid reader, every surface of JP's flat was covered in hardback books, including a copy of the John Irving novel *Until I Find You,* which features a tattoo artist and South Leith Parish Church graveyard. There was also a DVD of *T2,* the sequel to *Trainspotting,* on JP's table.

> *So, right, you should have a look yourself. Just be really confident, hold onto the window and put your head out and just look to the left and then look right. And I'll stand well away from you so I don't make you nervous.*

Stretched out in every direction was the best view I have ever seen of the capital city. From the sitting room window, facing south-east out to sea, I could see the Forth Estuary archipelago of its many inches – Inchmickery, Inchkeith, Inchgarvie, Inchcolm. And then the Bass Rock further east still, home to the world's largest colony of gannets and a Stevenson lighthouse. Sweeping my gaze east to west and fastening my steadfast grip of the window ledge, I could see the rolling Lammermuir hills clipping Berwick Law, Port Seton, Musselburgh and Portobello before the great hulking mass of Arthur's seat and the city loomed into view in the south west over my right shoulder.

Switching to JP's kitchen window, nearly the entire axis of Constitution Street could be seen, from the Foot of the Walk to the docks. It was a warm August evening and the city's pavements far below to the west were pulsing and steaming with the opening night shows of the Edinburgh Festival. Wax crayon bands of colour striped the summer sky – a sky filled with soaring gulls and neighbours hanging onto the edges of the sixteenth floor. The day melted as though it was the first and the last sunset I would ever know. I steadied myself, leaned back in and levered the window shut.

It's easy to get vertigo up here. I mean you can feel the building moving. It's got that classic thing where it moves in high winds. And you don't notice it. You have to sit very still. And then you'll notice that your curtains are moving. And then you think that's the wind. And then you notice it's not the wind. It's actually the building. It's just moving by a millimetre or two.

The building is approaching its fiftieth anniversary. Many other 1960s high-rise buildings – the 'multis' we called them in Dundee – have now been pulled down to make way for better quality, low-level housing, forever altering the urban skylines. JP doesn't think that Kirkgate House will be brought down anytime soon though, because a controlled demolition would be too hard to pull off in such a densely populated part of the city. I asked him about the impact of the Grenfell Tower fire and the response from local authorities in our own tale of two cities.

It was almost like panic, [the council] were putting something through our door every day. Although the exterior cladding is safe, we're not sure if the interior plywood which blocks off the older windows is safe. And there's only one way out. One set of stairs. In the Council cuts of 2016, they tried to take away our concierge and care-taking services but we all signed a petition. And there's no drug-dealing here anymore. There's very little anti-social behaviour – practically none.

Kirkgate House has been home to a diverse mix of neighbours over its fifty years. I have come to associate it with two encounters in particular, one involving the First Minister of Scotland and the other an alligator.

Firstly, the First Minister, once described by the *Daily Mail* as being the most dangerous woman in Britain.[12] I was taking Bonnie out for a lunchtime walk around the block, as I do every day. Except that, on this occasion in May 2017, Bonnie decided to stop abruptly for a pee on the grass verge outside Kirkgate House. As I stood waiting for her to finish, I noticed a shiny, maroon-coloured Jaguar with blacked out windows parked behind a loading bay. This isn't a typical car on Constitution Street so it caught my attention. I squinted my eyes to get a better look. At which point, the car windows were lowered and Nicola Sturgeon called out a cheery, almost neighbourly, *Hello! It's lovely to see you again.*

The First Minister began her career as a solicitor at Drumchapel Law Centre in Glasgow, advising local people on socio-economic rights including housing. On Constitution Street, she had been taking a brief pause on the General Election campaign trail in between an SNP rally at the Foot of the Walk and scheduled visits with local businesses. We chatted on the street for a while then I continued my lunchtime dog walk and she continued being the First Minister of Scotland.

And the story of the alligator? It is a story I heard about second-hand but it too was unexpected. In 2004, a resident of Kirkgate House was caught trying to sell the 4ft reptile from the boot of a car in the Kirkgate House car park after buying it over the internet and then realising that he could not care for it in his home. The man pleaded guilty at Edinburgh Sheriff Court to keeping a dangerous wild animal in the bathtub of his fifteenth floor flat and to recklessly endangering the lives of others including his neighbours.[13]

It is reasonable to assume that the man and the alligator took the lift up and down to the car park because fifteen floors of stairs is a long way to carry a snapping, female specimen weighing 7.5kg and regarded by wildlife experts as being very dangerous indeed. Not regularly serviced, according to some residents, the two lifts of Kirkgate House sometimes break down. For obvious reasons, our postman Craig prefers to take the lift to the top of the tower block each day and then run down delivering each flat's post. *But when the lift breaks, it certainly keeps you fit.* My neighbour JP once got stuck in the lift.

> *I got stuck in the lift with young parents and a baby. And we were stuck for fifty-five minutes. The guy kept kicking the doors of the lift. And I kept telling him to stop kicking the doors of the lift because it was not really going to help us. I said 'Look, I think we're going to get out of here in an hour' and he just said to me 'You shut the fuck up or I'll start kicking you!' So I was stuck in the lift with this giant, local guy, who I know to be a heavy-duty guy, telling me to shut the fuck up whilst I was trying to tell him to shut the fuck up so that we could both get a chance of getting out of there within an hour. We did get out within the hour. Fifty-five minutes to get out. But it was the worst excuse I've ever had in my life for going to a job interview late.*

JP has seen and heard a lot living in Kirkgate House. From his home immediately above the fifteenth floor, he recalled once hearing a muffled sound, much like the yelping of a distressed dog, coming from the central heating pipes that connect upper and lower flats.

Back down in the car park, the boot of a Vauxhall Cavalier was opened by undercover animal welfare officers who were confronted by an unrestrained and unmuzzled creature. A Kirkgate House resident explained that he had been looking for a pet and had come across the alligator for sale on the internet. He bought it for £250 from a man calling himself Bobby Brown.

Court reports state that our neighbour initially planned to keep the reptile in a 4ft fish tank at his flat in Kirkgate House, Constitution Street, believing the alligator to be only 12" long, and was said to have been quite taken aback by its actual size. The court heard he had fixed up a heating contraption which could have electrocuted the poor beast and was looking to buy a pond so he could keep it in his living room. The alligator, who doesn't appear to have been given a name, was fed on frozen mice and brown trout.

In sentencing, the sheriff said he was at a loss to come up with a punishment that would meet the stupidity and danger to others caused by the man's actions. The alligator was subsequently relocated to an animal sanctuary in South America. Some years later, the same neighbour was arrested for trying to smuggle a python out of a pet shop inside his trousers.

Contrary to what might be assumed from first sight and reputation of the tower block, the building is very popular with its current residents. It has the beneficial social ties highlighted by the UN Special Rapporteur on Housing. I asked JP about his immediate neighbours.

> *I'm proud to say that there are a couple of flats in this block that are solely for immigrants — short stay. They're becoming part of the fabric of this old building. We've got Venezuelans straight across from me, a single Mum on the right and a young couple with one child next door. Upstairs — a devout Polish Catholic family — go to Mass every night. Six kids under the age of seven. This is a proper mix of modern Leith. And they love their houses. House-proud in that kind of working class way of being proud of the neighbourhood.*

Being house-proud is part of being known and belonging to a place. Small, everyday occurrences of familiarity, like those described by JP, can make us feel grounded and at home. The cognitive limit to the number of people with whom one person can apparently maintain a stable social relationship is said to be somewhere between 100 and 250, with a commonly used value of 150, referred to as Dunbar's Number.[14] 150 was the basic unit of professional armies in ancient Rome, the estimated size of a Neolithic farming village, and also approximately the number of street numbers on Constitution Street (depending on whether or not industrial units are counted). A city of streets has the potential to be a collective of inter-connected, social webs. This isn't always the reality, however.

In her book *The Lonely City* author Olivia Laing explores a city's uneasy combination of separateness and exposure, as experienced from the solitude of her New York apartment and the disembodying effects of social media community.[15] She describes the cumulative pangs of anxiety experienced when loneliness becomes harder to hide from those around you. The crisis of intimacy in Laing's New York is replicated in the gathering shame spreading around the door frames and phone screens of lonely dwellers in cities and streets across the world.

Of course, loneliness and social isolation is not only a contemporary affliction. For the German-born Jewish American political theorist, Hannah Arendt, belonging to a community and being visible in everyday civic space had a direct correlation not only to personal wellbeing but on the ability to promote and protect the rights of others. She believed that in the 1930s, citizens were primed for the appeal of totalitarian leaders because they were isolated from any community, political or otherwise. The experience of the Holocaust demonstrated that 'human dignity needed a new guarantee.'[16]

Human rights law was that new guarantee. The right to adequate housing is the right to accessible, affordable and available shelter. It was first included in The Universal Declaration of Human Rights 1948 and then in The International Covenant on Economic, Social and Cultural Rights 1966,[17] as well as in many subsequent national constitutions around the world.

For example, the right to housing was included in the Constitution of the Republic of South Africa 1996.[18] Post-apartheid South Africa may seem like unlikely terrain for establishing international precedents in constitutional law but some of the most advanced deliberations on human dignity, equality and freedom took root in the courtroom in the early days of the new democracy. A South African Constitutional Court case from 2000 on the right to housing is one of the cases most referenced in other jurisdictions.[19]

The respondent in the case, Mrs Grootboom, had been evicted from her informal home situated on private land earmarked for building formal, low-cost housing. The case held that the state has a duty to provide appropriate shelter, within its available resources, for people who have no roof at all over their heads because of eviction, fire or floods. Known as 'the right to live under the stars' case, Mrs Grootboom died never having moved from her shack to a brick house.[20] The fact that her family were still without reasonable accommodation, despite the Constitutional Court ruling in her favour, showed how difficult it was to realise the socio-economic rights in the constitution without corresponding resourcing and prioritising the rights of the most vulnerable and marginalised in society.

In a unanimous judgment, the judges of the South African Constitutional Court held that treating people as human beings should be the determinant of the reasonableness of state action. The fundamental value of human dignity, including having basic shelter, was held to be the cornerstone of applying the constitution in practice.

The right to housing does not have similar constitutional protection in the UK. While the UK has signed the relevant international treaties, the rights have not been incorporated into our domestic legal framework and so are not easily enforceable in court. When I asked neighbours for their views on this gap, the response was mixed. For instance, my neighbour James, an architect, was very sceptical:

I don't think we have a right to anything. If you want a house, you go and earn it. I don't think there's any good reason why people are homeless. I do think that there's definitely a Lazy-British — you know, there are some people who just think they should get money from the Government and I don't think that's right.

Perceptions of getting and giving money strike at the heart of the relationship between the state and its citizens and a rights-based approach versus a hierarchy of power and privilege. Should a country's tax system be a social-democratic model that favours high public spend on social security or one that is driven by market forces and free choice?

Built in 1815 and known as the Georgian House or the Waterloo Buildings, 134–138 Constitution Street was formerly the sheriff office occupied by a debt collection agency on behalf of local government. This was where the hugely unpopular Community Charge or Poll Tax, first piloted in Scotland by the Thatcherite Conservative Government, was enforced on those who couldn't, or wouldn't, pay.

My neighbour Rob remembers standing in line to pay the Poll Tax in person at the Constitution Street sheriff office. He told me that his refusal to give authorities his postal address was his personal act of protest. He caused disruption in the line by encouraging other Leithers settling debts to also refuse to give authorities personal data.

The same building where Rob protested is now residential flats and home to homeopathic practitioner and doula, Robyn. She told me that she first moved to the street in 1993 and, at that time, lived opposite the old debt-collection offices. She remembers regularly hearing the windows opposite being smashed.

The Right to Housing

As often as once a week, someone would put a brick through the windows.
People were angry at having had their homes repossessed.

Today, levels of inequality across health, education, housing, and child poverty affect one in five families in Scotland.[21] In the Leith area where I live, it is one in four families who live in poverty.[22] We appear to be living in a Victorian era, albeit with less philanthropy.

One of only two statues of women in the city, the Queen Victoria memorial stands at the west of Constitution Street. Commemorating Victoria's visit to Leith in 1842, its unveiling in 1907 was said to have been watched by a crowd of over 20,000 people. The memorial was subsequently moved in 1985 and again in 2003 for cleaning. When first uprooted, a glass casket was discovered containing local newspapers from 1907 along with coins and other memorabilia. The contents of the casket were replaced along with a copy of the *Edinburgh Evening News*, a set of newly minted coins and a videotape from a BBC Scotland documentary about the redevelopment of Leith.

Thinking of this, and my parents gift to me in 1982, I asked neighbours about what we could include in a street time capsule from our lives today, to be buried under the tarmac when Constitution Street is dug open once more for extension of the Edinburgh trams project. My neighbour Mary, landlady of the old Port O' Leith pub since 1982, suggested putting some memorabilia from the bar into a time capsule.

I've got the figurehead from the bar. Of course, it's got my face on it so not much good to anybody else, ha! It's lying on top of my wardrobe and honestly it hasn't even been dusted or washed since I brought it home from the pub eight years ago. Oh, that's terrible!

Our domestic lives side by side on a street are about seeing people up close and vulnerable, full of our dusty, unwashed honesties and hamely fare. Providing shelter for ourselves and our families is about basic survival needs. Home life, and therefore housing, is inherently personal. Threat of rent-hikes, forced eviction or general neglect of public housing stock are attacks on human dignity with often little legal remedy. This perhaps explains why housing rights mobilisation, in the form of organised protest and the establishment of housing cooperatives in a city, is often the first cause taken up by today's activists that will go onto become tomorrow's civic leaders.

The city of Edinburgh is expected to have the highest population growth in Scotland over the next twenty years.[23] This growth will strain existing housing and public services unless more is done. While Scottish law and policy already includes some housing rights, there are big gaps. Incorporating the right to housing into domestic law, as part of an adequate standard of living, in a written constitution, would fill many of these gaps and progress putting rights into practice. Now and in the future of housing on this street and every other street, we will need more active participation of rights holders – current and prospective residents – in the decision-making process about how our housing is planned for.

At the end of my road, in the space where there should be a view of the sea – the same sea which first brought wealth to the city and which will one day reclaim the land – there is instead a casino and a car park. The neon strip-lighting of the casino sign blocks out any view of the sea. We have to take the lift up sixteen floors of Kirkgate House to properly get the full sea vista.

My city's trashing of its coastline is a form of civic and natural vandalism and the lack of urban planning a kind of madness. For too long, private property investment has been championed at the expense of social housing and helping people buy a house to live in. With any real luck, our housing stock will one day be celebrated as homes and will be fully affordable, accessible and habitable for all. They will be strong, safe and secure enough to outlast us. After all, we belong to the street and the street belongs to us, for the moment in time in which we call it home. Peace of mind is knowing that where we lay our head at night is a place we can linger long.

Everyone has the right to a standard of living adequate for the health and well-being of himself and of his family, including food, clothing, housing and medical care and necessary social services, and the right to security in the event of unemployment, sickness, disability, widowhood, old age or other lack of livelihood in circumstances beyond his control...

Article 25, The Universal Declaration of Human Rights

Yeah, I'm alright, pal. Same old, same old.

Sajit, Corner Shop Owner, 30 Constitution Street

The Right to Food

Companionship

FOOD BANK USE AT RECORD HIGH

**BREXIT IS A RED HERRING WHEN
IT COMES TO FISHING**

**MUMS HOARD MONTHS OF FOOD AND
MEDICINE IN PREPARATION FOR BREXIT**

MIGRANT LABOUR CRISIS!

The billboard outside the corner shop spells out its headlines like a placard at Speaker's Corner. Inside, the newsagent's shelves bear an altogether calmer burden of everyday convenience items – sweets, alcohol, pet food, cigarettes and sliced, white bread. Standing chatting to owner, Sajit, I have learnt about my street's many food cultures from observing what he rings up on the till. The diversity of dishes, where we eat, when and who with, all reflect the mix of people at home here and says something too about what we want to bring with us and to leave behind from previous homes near and far. The stories about who we share our daily bread with speak about community.

Food poverty and food insecurity are human rights issues.[1] According to volunteers at the Edinburgh North East Food Bank – a network of over 200 agencies who refer people in need of support – almost a third of people in my area don't have enough to eat on a daily basis.[2] This is the same area that has several Michelin star restaurants.

For those who do have enough to eat at home, many of us eat our meals alone. Both living alone through choice and experiencing social isolation and loneliness are increasing across the age spectrum.[3] Companionship, to be in company, comes from the Latin *companio,* one who eats bread (*pane*) with you. As with the Lord's Prayer, it is not give *me* my daily bread. It is give *us* our daily bread. Eating and community go together in the knowing of one another. The best of my street conversations were had while sharing food with neighbours in their homes and cafés.

For example, I picked thyme leaves with Reyhan as she prepared the lunchtime salad orders in her café. A one-hour recorded interview with a neighbour typically took about three or four hours to transcribe word by word, slowly and carefully picking the exact letters from my keyboard like the harvesting of these delicate, precise leaves from a twig of thyme scenting the air. Reyhan is Kurdish and the café sells a mixture of her and husband Icout's traditional spinach and feta cheese *borek*, along with Scottish soups, baked potatoes and, their speciality, homemade baklava that drips with honey and pistachio nuts.

Lunchtime is a sociable time of day on Constitution Street. Further along from the cafés, Linda's Snax Van has been parked outside the former entrance to the docks on the street for twenty years. The Snax Van is a white box on wheels resembling an aid agency portacabin in a disaster zone. It sits nestled in between bramble weeds and wiry seed pods of broom. Linda herself radiates good health. Tanned and smiling, she sits reading in a deck chair outside the van. Then during the peak fry-up hours of late morning until early afternoon, Linda appears in a pinny, propped up on her elbows behind the service hatch of the white box. Her lunchtime customers queuing up for snacks of lorne sausage rolls and mugs of tea sweetened with refined sugar, used to all be dockers. Now, they are graphic designers, estate agents and marketing consultants.

Sugar was also big business for Leith in the eighteenth century. Leith merchants set sail across the seas from the docks at the foot of the street to the world beyond. They traded directly with slave plantations producing sugar and tobacco. Sir John Gladstone, father of Prime Minister William Gladstone, was a Leith merchant who made his fortune from owning slaves across nine plantations. When slaves were freed under the Slavery Abolition Act 1833, Gladstone senior received a compensation payment from the British Government equating to £83million in today's money. None of this is written on the historical plaque marking the former Leith home of the Gladstones near Constitution Street.

In December 1786, at the same time as Edinburgh town planners sought parliamentary approval for a new thoroughfare to be named Constitution Street, an Ayrshire farmer and aspiring poet with mounting debts bought a ticket to sail on The Roselle ship from Leith to Jamaica. As a book-keeper on a sugar plantation in the West Indies, Robert Burns would have become complicit in the full horror of the slave trade that made many Scottish merchants and seamen wealthy. My own ancestor, Captain James Smith, who sailed on voyages from Timberbush (from *bourse,* the exchange of timber), Leith, at around the same time, made note in his memoirs of 'that other trade for which I do not wish to be associated.'[4]

At the eleventh hour, Burns found an Edinburgh publisher for his *Poems, Chiefly in the Scottish Dialect,* cancelled his ticket aboard The Roselle and, so it goes, the rest is history. His later song *The Slave's Lament,*[5] written in 1792, hints at a knowledge of the other trade:

Torn from that lovely shore,
and must never see it more;
And alas! I am weary, weary O.

The current regulars queuing for sugary tea from Linda at her Snax Van include office workers from the Creative Exchange co-working space next door. Formerly a corn exchange, the building is wrapped in a ribbon of sandstone frieze depicting renaissance cherubs, known as the 'Leith babies'. The chubby babies are merrily gathering corn, loading the corn onto ships, picking grapes and getting drunk on jugs of French claret. I have admired these cherubs or putti after the building was converted into a co-working space and it became my office. Every day, I walk the short commute of two blocks from my tenement flat in the middle of the street to the eastern axis at no. 29, the Creative Exchange. Within, the grand hall is buttressed like a gothic cathedral by curving, pine trusses, ornate iron gusset infills and gold leaf.

Built in 1861 as a marketing hall, the Corn Exchange was later a depot for a scaffolding company, an occasional venue for tall ship celebrations and the headquarters of the Northern Lighthouse Board. The Victorian extension to the right of the hall retains wooden bannisters topped by twin painted lighthouses that hint at the past. The insignia of the Scottish Corn Association is also visible from sepia-tinted photographs of my tenement building in the nineteenth century, when the offices of the Association were located here. Looking at these photographs made me realise that the morning commute along Constitution Street had been a well-trodden path for merchants, producers and administrators for centuries.

In the eighteenth and nineteenth centuries, most towns in the UK had a corn or grain exchange, corn being the generic term for all cereal grain varieties, not only maize as in North America. At the end of the nineteenth century, the independent burgh of Leith had five flour mills and several grain elevators at the dry docks. The elevators sucked grain out of the holds of ships and deposited it onto the quay to take to ware-houses, where it was then stored in silos ready for shipment by railroad to mills, breweries and distilleries across the country. Now condemned for demolition, the Imperial Grain Elevator beyond Constitution Street used to grind 6,000 sacks of flour per week and employ more than 200 people.

Before approaching the empty grain silo, the first and last dwelling of the street is the former Gatehouse for Leith Docks. Now a private home, the triangular roof of the gatehouse brings to mind a miniature Swiss chalet atop a wind-up music box. Its alpine meadows are in fact a housing development from the 1980s and a small roundabout leading to the casino. As well as functioning as the reception for workers clocking in and out from shifts at the docks, the Gatehouse also once housed a ratcatcher's office. I can guess that at some later point the building became a fruit importer's office because, when renovating, the current owner found an invoice book from 1946 which listed exotic fruit orders of peaches and pineapples for the big hotels in central Edinburgh. The line of small shacks selling fruit at the entrance to the docks became known as Banana Row.

Exotic fruit is one of the few things not on the menu at Pierinos Fish and Chip Shop on the corner of Constitution Street. Fish suppers, haggis suppers, pies, pizzas and the infamous Scottish deep-fried Mars bar are all popular choices. I am a regular customer on a Friday night, when Bonnie and I enjoy a fish supper.

Brothers Adriano and Domenico are part of the Crolla dynasty of Italian food connoisseurs renowned in Edinburgh for their delicatessens, cafés and cookery books. Parents Pierino and Lucia began the fish and chip shop business in 1983, coinciding with the closure of the last shipyard in Leith, Henry Robb Ltd., which brought an end to over 600 years of shipbuilding in the area. Adriano told me about helping in the shop from the age of twelve, lifting sacks of potatoes into the chipping machine and serving customers. The brothers' sister, Lora, owns the beautician next door, and the next generation of Crollas are now being trained up for the family business.

Yeah, we bring them in. They've got to learn where we make our money, you know, how we pay for things.

I once forgot my purse when ordering my Friday night takeaway. Adriano reassured me with a familial warmth, *You're alright, we ken you.* And they do ken their local kith and kin.

The customers in the 1980s and '90s were dockers, sailors and lorry drivers and the shop was busier on a Monday night than on a Friday night. It was with a mix of fondness and exasperation that I heard the Crollas recall the past, making customers sound like long-lost, eccentric relatives at an Italian family wedding.

Och, customers, ha ha! Well, we also had another place back in early '90s and the customers then were a lot more, erm, interesting, than the ones that used to come in here, because it was right next to Cables Wynd House.

Cables Wynd House is known locally as the Banana Flats due to the distinctive curved shape. The flats were immortalised in Irvine Welsh's *Trainspotting* in which they are the childhood home of character Simon 'Sick Boy' Williamson, friend and accomplice to Renton, Begbie and Spud. Notorious in the 1980s for being at the centre of Leith's heroin epidemic, the flats have now been given Category A status by Historic Environment Scotland, rating them alongside Edinburgh Castle, the Forth Rail Bridge and the Royal Botanic Garden Edinburgh.

As I stood chatting to Adriano at the chip shop counter, I realised that Pierinos supplied the spuds for Leith's own anti-hero, Spud. A trio of workmen in overalls and steel-capped boots then came through the door and ordered a lunchtime mix of pies, sausages and chips, washed down with a two-litre bottle of Irn Bru. Adriano didn't hesitate in dousing the men's chips liberally with the brown sauce favoured by those with local accents. We then turned our conversation to something far less predictable at the time – Brexit.[6]

Support for leaving the EU was popular among those connected to the fishing industry in Scotland due to long-held frustrations with fishing quotas and territorial disputes with foreign vessels off the Scottish coast. However, the price of fish was not what was making Adriano anxious.

> *Yeah, all the talk of war and stuff, it seems like it's just around the corner. You know with Mr Trump and North Korea. And the Brexit thing is just going to cause more division I think. It's going back instead of forward. Scotland? I'd like Scotland to be independent but financially I don't think they could cope on their own, especially the way the oil business is at the moment.*

I picked him up on his use of 'they'. Dressed in a black Gucci polo shirt with an Italian tricolore on the collar, Adriano identifies as Scots Italian. Born and bred in Edinburgh, he proudly showed me a picture on his phone of the rolling green hills of the Picinisco area between Rome and Naples where most of the Edinburgh Italians originate from. Adriano's father, Pierino Crolla, arrived in Edinburgh aged just nineteen in the 1960s. He worked as a farm labourer in the Niddrie area before establishing the family business in Leith with wife Lucia. In the language of today's tabloid press, he was an economic migrant in search of a better life.

The ultimate foodie test of where you call home is whether you prefer salt n' sauce or salt n' vinegar on your chips. Being of an inclusive and generous nature, Adriano admits to putting all three – salt, brown sauce and vinegar – on his own chips and insists that the fish has to be haddock and not cod.

I go by accents now when I'm asking people what they want. Years ago, because there were so many lorry drivers and sailors and they were often English, we always used vinegar.

If the past is a foreign country, then the street and its go-between inhabitants are changing, as they always have done. Throughout history, there have been waves of immigration and emigration to and from this gateway to the wider world.

Further along the street, I chatted to Gabrielle, owner of the Hideout Café. As if on cue, Bob Dylan's 'The Times They Are Changin'' could be heard playing from a second-hand cassette player. Gabrielle is originally from the Czech Republic and her husband, Hasan, from Albania. Their young children have Scottish accents and, like many families that have made Scotland their new home, they are supportive of what they term Scotland's right to self-determination.

To be honest, I am quite happy for Scotland to become independent because I feel that they have tried a lot being part of the Union and I don't think they are benefiting as much as England is trying to convince them. So I think that it's time they should do things by themselves and I would fully support that…I think there's lots of fear for some reason. But I think it's just a fear of being inferior. I think it depends on how people pull together.

Gabrielle and Hasan's busy café on Constitution Street was once a drysalters. This maritime-grocer and ironmonger sold everything needed for a long voyage at sea, from paraffin lamps to brooms and brass tacks. It's possible that my own sea-faring ancestor, Captain Smith, shopped for supplies here.

After its last incarnation as a Chinese takeaway, the shop lay empty for a decade.

It was in really bad shape but we saw potential and we had a really good feeling about the area and we went for it. There are so many neighbours that we know personally. We know where they work, what they do, about their lives.

With a degree in architecture, preserving the history of the shop was important to Gabrielle. The new place has also gained a reputation outside of the local area for vintage music thanks to its collection of second-hand cassette tapes. The family are invested in making Scotland their forever-home after having lived in several different European countries. I asked Gabrielle if she had encountered any anti-immigrant discrimination since the Brexit vote.

Not directly with me. People are more like, 'oh my god, I'm so sorry that, you know, Brexit happened.' I still feel welcome. I mean my five-year-old can make some sort of sense of things already. He speaks Scottish. You know, that's what he says. At nursery, there's no 'Oh he's Czech and Albanian'. No, he's just Scottish.

The choice of food is as diverse as the people that live and work on the street. I heard a rumour that Pierinos fish and chip shop was formerly a bakers. *Yeah, that's right, Martin's the Bakers,* confirmed Adriano. *Actually, we used the old bread mixer for our pizza dough so I suppose it's all connected.*

Like the resting, warming phase for bread or pizza dough, I think that the current in between time for constitutional change in Scotland, the UK and Europe will one day be looked back upon as a kind of proving phase. We are in a moment when we need to ask ourselves fundamental questions about what kind of place we want to live in and who we want to have companionship with. The right to food is not realised for everyone in Scotland today.

The stories I heard of different food cultures mixing together led me and my taste buds along the street like a trail of breadcrumbs or pizza crust. When neighbours told me about the repurposing of former haunts into new culinary destinations, I learnt about how Scotland's population is changing and about how that should be reflected in a written constitution. Scottish food is Italian, Czech, Albanian, Kurdish, Pakistani, and much more. I am hopeful that today's newspaper headlines in the corner shop about fear and division will be wrapping tomorrow's fish supper at the chippie.

Everyone has the right to a standard of living adequate for the health and well-being of himself and of his family, including food, clothing, housing and medical care and necessary social services, and the right to security in the event of unemployment, sickness, disability, widowhood, old age or other lack of livelihood in circumstances beyond his control...

Article 25, The Universal Declaration of Human Rights

If you went somewhere to buy heroin and they didn't have it, you could get it within a two-minute walk of that door. And then of course the AIDS thing happened and wiped out a generation.

Ritchie, Tattooist, 177 Constitution Street

The Right to Health

Closing Time

What does it mean to lead a healthy life? Can it be both a long life and a good life? And what role does the body politic have in progressing the right to health? These were the interconnecting questions that I kept in mind as I left the chip shop queue for a deeper dive into Leith and the embodied experience of decision-making.

Around the corner from my street, the old Leith hospital became the first in the country to accept female medical students and it was here, in 1832, that the first intravenous treatment for cholera was given. However, for generations Constitution Street was synonymous with poverty-related ill health and low life expectancy compared with more affluent areas of the city.

The human right to health is not a right to be healthy. Genetics and varied lifestyle make this impossible. It is instead a right to the full range of services, care and information which are needed for physical and mental health and wellbeing. Health inequalities persist on Constitution Street and this is symptomatic of the broader picture across Scotland.[1] It is a case history involving drink, drugs and depression. The more positive news is that it is also a story about courage and recovery.

A good place to pick up the story is at last orders in the pub. On a Saturday night in April 2017, my heart and glass were full at the Port O' Leith pub's closing down party. The old bar at 58 Constitution Street was an institution for supporters of local football club, Hibs. I live next door and have had a conflicted relationship with this neighbour. The Port O' Leith was here on the street long before me but I don't always want to hear local anthem 'Sunshine on Leith' being sung at such a high volume, out of tune, that it makes my window panes shake. It was therefore with mixed emotions that I joined neighbours at the bar's last chorus. The party was already in full swing when we arrived.

Poppers. It's only poppers! Will you no try some? Gie you a head-rush.

'Nah, you're alright,' I said, declining. One friend shrugged. Another inhaled. *One more tune! One more tune!* Our heels anchored into the foam beneath the ripped, leather bench on which we swayed. Back and forth. Sweat dripping, tears streaming, arms flailing, hair slapping, thirsting, and pulsing with joy. And sorrow. A sorrow for all that had gone before in the bar and never would be again. For absent friends. For kindness and beauty. And for the here and now, in between, at last orders. Because there wasn't going to be another round at the old Port O' Leith bar.

The lads with the poppers were bare-chested *taps aff*, lassoing empties with someone's green and white Hibs shirt, checking that we noticed their aim and their hit rate. A trio of old-timers bumped and grinded against the steel-barred window frames to the rhythm of Madness', 'Our House', followed by an obligatory 'Hey Jude'. Sad songs made better.

A man I recognised as my window cleaner, Dougie, straightened and smoothed his long, blonde wig before ringing a ship's brass bell behind the bar majestically to call last orders. A barmaid was wide-eyed and greetin' in the corner. Soft dancing and hard drinking landed all around us on the chequerboard floor tiles. Everything stuck. Half of a 'No football colours, No trackies' note was stuck to the side of a table leg. The ladies' toilets were out of order. And then there was Mary. Elegant and instantly recognisable in her long, leopard-print coat, diamante-studded slippers and coiffed hair, pinned à la Bet Lynch. The former landlady offered a regal wave to the regulars. *Plenty of queens in the pub tonight*, she said, winking.

The bar had a reputation far and wide. Foreign coins from visiting sailors across the world were sellotaped onto the interior walls next to photographs of regulars. Che Guevara and Saltire flags were drawn together like theatre drapes suspended from the ceiling. The morning after the closing party, these flags, coins and photographs were torn down. Number 58 Constitution Street was put out of its misery by a squad of renovation henchmen. The old limbs of red timber, wonky bar stools and scratched mirrors were hacked off and seized as props by the newly gentrified Leith of coffee shops and design studios. And I was complicit in the cultural appropriation. I salvaged the mirror from the ladies' toilets as a gift for Maddie, across the road.

When the lights came on for the last time at closing, it was time to get our coats. I surveyed the structural and human wreckage at the end of the night and as we searched high and low for her black, leather jacket, my neighbour and friend told me that, now twenty years sober, there was once a time when she hadn't expected to outlive the old boozer. The jacket was eventually found hidden behind the bar. It hadn't been stolen, as I feared, but put there by another neighbour to prevent it from getting dirty on the dancefloor.

'Yeah, yeah, yeah, yeah', faded the last words of the chorus to 'Sunshine on Leith' for the final time as we stumbled home. The light of the sky was also changing. Gulls from the docks circled overhead like pterodactyls from a lost, maritime valley. Older neighbours had told me before that circling gulls are a warning sign of an approaching storm. The birds swooped and cackled and gathered in number like a marauding army of avian soldiers high on chips and sweet, brown sauce. They were lusting for a scrap outside the bar and pointed and jabbed their beaks into the messy aftermath of the party.

The street, like Scotland itself, has always had a messy relationship with alcohol. When first laid out in 1790 as a new thoroughfare connecting sea and city, the street was baptised with booze. When there was no fresh, running water, people drank ale, or wine if they could afford it. Throughout much of the preceding century, England (and then Britain from 1707) had been at war with France and trade in French wine was consequently restricted. Enterprising Scots had been able to sell on the claret that arrived into Leith docks at a profit to their English neighbours.

A masonry detail on a bay window ledge behind the Port O' Leith shows the head of Dionysus, also known as Bacchus, wreathed in vines flanked by shields bearing the initials of whisky bond owners. This is the Greco-Roman god of theatre, fertility, ritual madness and wine. Often shown to be androgynous in youthful appearance, Dionysus is the perfect pin-up for liminal times and places.

Today, Scotland is only just beginning to sober up from the ritual madness of drinking. Regarded as the sick-man of Europe, twenty-two people a week die of alcohol-related illness.[2] In 2017, the UK Supreme Court held in favour of the Scottish Government's plans for minimum alcohol pricing, rejecting an appeal by the Scotch Whisky Association and upholding right to health arguments.[3]

The other chronic ill-health affliction for my neighbours is smoking. Smoking-related illness accounts for a fifth of all deaths in Scotland.[4] While not without its critics when first introduced in 2006, the ban on smoking in enclosed public spaces has helped cut cases of stroke and heart disease.

My neighbour Max is seventy-three and has smoked all his life. He phoned me from his bedside in hospital.

Hi babe. It's me. I need you to come and get me. I've been really unlucky again and am stuck in hospital.

Max laid down the phone receiver and I could hear him croak hoarsely to a nurse:

Yeah, that's Jemma, my neighbour. She's a lawyer. Very reliable. She has a car.

I tried to interrupt at the end of the phone, explaining that I'm not a real lawyer, that my car certainly isn't reliable, and that I'm not his 'babe', but it seemed futile. I got my keys and went to collect my neighbour and friend from hospital.

Max has been in and out of hospital with chronic obstructive pulmonary disease. Given the range and amount of different narcotics he has smoked, bad luck has little to do with his recurrent hospital admissions. When well enough, he liked to walk up and down Constitution Street each day, *just cruising* as he put it. Originally from Nigeria, Max has lived in the UK for over forty years but still finds the Leith climate harsh. No matter the weather, he dresses in a duffle coat and beanie hat for his daily constitutional. His politics are consistently off-beat too. Max told me that he thinks there is far too much immigration in Scotland and that he regards President Trump in the US as a role model for family values, such is the President's close bond with his children. Max doesn't keep in touch with his own sons.

Despite our different politics, I offered to drive Max the short distance to the polling station on General Election Day on 8 June 2017 to ensure that he exercised his right to vote. It was the snap General Election, called by Prime Minister Theresa May to try to strengthen her hand in Brexit negotiations – a tactic which backfired spectacularly when the Conservatives lost their majority at the polls and could only form a government propped up by ten members of the Northern Ireland Democratic Unionist Party.

We arrived at the polling station inside the primary school at 9.50pm. As the midsummer dusk began to close in around us, there was ten minutes to spare until the close of polls. Max emerged from the voting booth, his walking stick raised triumphantly in the air, exclaiming, *I'm an elector!*

The political weather was hot and unsettled the following day and Constitution Street was no different. The pavement slabs were warm to touch and the cafés were full. Yet some things stayed the same. I came across Max wearing his coat, hat and gloves and sitting on the stone wall opposite the Burns statue. A hearse passed by on its way to the nearby crematorium. *Wait, taxi!* he shouted. *Eee, Jemma, I'm still here!*

Ever the joker, about nine out of ten things Max told me I believe to be true. I believe that in the 1960s, he met Fela Kuti's son, Femi, and together they embarked on the hippie trail overland to India in search of good quality hashish. I believe that in the 1970s, Max shared a flat on Drummond Street in Edinburgh with David Bowie. I believe that in the early 1980s, he came back from the dead after being beaten up by racist police officers inside the former cells of the Constitution Street station. A doctor at the mortuary noticed his toes twitching and pulled him out from the freezer.

However, despite all that he told me, I am not entirely convinced that for much of the 1980s Max worked as a bouncer in Nobles on Constitution Street when the pub was a strip club. I am not certain because I don't know how he could have fitted in all the drugs and rock and roll while holding down a full-time job. His job apparently involved stopping punters from getting too close to the topless women, the so-called 'go-go dancers', in the windows.

Nobles was first opened in 1896 by whisky bonder and wine merchant, Archibald Noble, and the pub retains its original stained-glass panelling depicting the Leith crest and motto, 'Persevere', that shows the Virgin Mary, or perhaps Mary Magdalene, and a baby in a boat at sea. Unlike all the other Persevere emblems I have seen in stained glass windows, the version in Nobles does not have a protective cloud above the boat but, rather, rays of sunshine. So here, I think, is the original sunshine on Leith.[5]

Nobles is now a family-run gastro pub owned by artists Fay and Niall. I chatted to the couple about their experience of starting a business during the economic recession and of being gradually accepted by the pub's older clientele.

It was pretty dangerous and rough round here in its heyday but the bars and the pubs were a safe haven for people to come into. There was a commu-nity element. And that's what we wanted to retain.

Landlady of the neighbouring Port O' Leith in the rougher days, Mary, is of the same generation as my neighbour Max. In the 1980s, when Mary and Max were working in the pubs and clubs of the street, Mary's bar had a 6am license to serve dockers and ships crews. I asked her about her experiences serving alcohol in a male-dominated environment.

A man would take a swipe at another man but even drunk men were reti-cent to take a swipe at me. Anyway, I would have swiped 'em right back! That sounds like a toughy thing but I had plenty of backup.

Mary recalled her customers running up the street at closing time to catch sight of the *dancing girls* in Nobles. Some of the women dancing were as young as fifteen or sixteen years old and I struggled to share in her glow of nostalgia. The pub was also where actor Robbie Coltrane made his acting debut in an advert for Tennent's Lager which featured lap-dancing. Changing Nobles' seedier reputation was a priority for Fay on taking on the pub in 2010:

> *Memories of the pub weren't always positive ones. Especially in regard to women and how women were treated in here. I think that was very relevant for me being a so-called landlady. Men would be standing at the bar commenting on my breasts like I wasn't there. Old guys will mention the magical days of the lap dancers, the girls in cages or what have you and we just sort of laugh it off. It's part of the history of the place. But people have to realise that times have changed. Especially in regard to how women are perceived in this industry. That has to be a big shift.*

For some, the dancing girls in Nobles and pubs like it provided harmless entertainment and light relief during a period shaped by high unemployment, addiction and violence. For me, it is one example of the deep-rooted misogyny in our local psyche that is best consigned to the past.

When I talked with Mary in her home about change and loss on the street, I noticed that she used the past and present tenses interchangeably. A willowy figure, she had a mischievous, girlish glint in her eye that twinkled like the diamantes on her studded slippers. Pausing to stub out her cigarette in an ashtray on the kitchen table, she showed me photographs of her twin sister, Elizabeth, also with blonde hair piled regally high on her head, who lives in Dallas, Texas.

Mary herself is glamorous in the original meaning of the old Scots word – beguiling and bewitching. She likes a vodka soda and claims not to suffer from hangovers. When I first sketched out my street research plans, I sought out Mary's permission as the elder matriarch of the street and she gave me her blessing. I asked her how she felt about being anointed by locals as Mary Queen of Leith.

It's a lovely compliment but then you must understand that when I stand behind a bar and serve drinks to people, they all know me. I was once collecting my grandson from school — he was about ten years old at the time — we were walking down the street and a few men that were walking in the other direction shouted out 'Hello, Mary!' My grandson said to me, 'Granny, how do you know so many men?' I told him the truth — it's cause I work in the pub.

When I interviewed Mary in March 2018, news from the wider world at the time spoke of Russian agents attempting to murder a former spy in Britain using a chemical nerve agent. Russian diplomats were swiftly expelled from the UK and Russia retaliated with counter measures. Relations between Russia and Western Europe had not been so frosty since Soviet Union times and the Cold War.

When the Soviet Union collapsed in 1991, Latvian sailors aboard a Soviet ship docked in Leith found themselves run aground without the means to return home, the Russian Embassy having refused to pay the ship's docking fees. The sailors arrived on the street on 1 April (not a coincidence according to Mary) and didn't get back home until Christmas. In the interim, they had to rely on the goodwill of local people to help them. However, two of the ship's crew, both called Sergei, chose to linger in Leith into the new year before stowing away on a ship bound for America.

Mary recalled the two Sergeis fondly. Working in the pub for thirty years, she served many sailors from across the world. The bar was brought to further international recognition in the novel and subsequent film about heroin addiction, *Trainspotting*, in which the bar was called Port Sunshine. *Trainspotting* takes its name from the derelict train station at the crossroads of Constitution Street and Leith Walk where character Francis Begbie comes across his alcoholic, vagabond father.

On the same spot today stands a GP's surgery and three pharmacies. Scotland still has the highest number of drug-related deaths in Europe. My cousin is a GP in the surgery. She told me that doctors still issue opiate prescriptions everyday but drug addiction is not nearly as visible on the street as it once was.

My neighbour Ritchie remembers when drugs were on every corner of the street and the tragic consequences of a lack of public health awareness.

> *Back in the '80s, heroin just destroyed this place. You know, there probably wasnae anybody under the age of twenty doon here that wasnae actually on that kind of drugs. Because it was so easy to get… Then of course the AIDS thing happened and wiped out a generation.*

The rate of HIV/AIDS was particularly high amongst heroin users in the 1980s because of the sharing of needles. One of Ritchie's school friends was the first man in Scotland to die of AIDS, aged about eighteen or nineteen at the time, according to Ritchie.

> *There was hardly anybody it never touched. You know, entire families, generations, it went through them all. And it still lives on today. It's maybe not as rife as it was but it's still there.*

The stigma associated with HIV/AIDS has lessened in the last three decades with greater public health awareness and access to antiretroviral medicines. However, a shaming silence still shrouds much ill-health on the street. This shame manifests itself in people being reluctant to talk honestly about health or to seek out healthcare.

Prescribing antidepressants keeps my cousin and her colleagues in the surgery particularly busy. I sometimes bumped into neighbours queuing, like me, at the pharmacy for prescriptions and while we kept a confidential distance, it was as though we pretended not to know one another until back outside when the response to 'how are you?' was the standard 'yeah fine, not bad.' Things were clearly not fine.

When asking searching questions of my neighbours, I thought it only fair that I also opened up about how I was feeling at the time. To do so meant acknowledging my privilege – privilege that includes access to information that comes from education, being warm and dry in my damp-free flat and being well-fed thanks to the spending power of salaried employment. Yet despite all of this, I still felt really shitty on some days. Having access to healthcare and the confidence with which to seek it out meant that I could choose to do something about it.

Observing my own mood, I noticed how many of us walk with our shoulders hunched, stooping against the cold wind and also, perhaps, hiding within our anxious selves. The experience of being walled off within a city's grid of streets can combine with a sense of near-unbearable claustrophobia. Like many Scots, I experience that hemmed-in feeling most during the winter months when it is harder to obtain enough vitamin D from sunlight. In an effort to counter the effects of seasonal depression, I took up membership at a community gym. The exercise boosted my endorphin-levels of course, but I believe I benefitted more from the new friendships I formed through the commitment of a class timetable.

Based out of an empty shop unit behind the street, the Projekt 42 community gym aims to be as inclusive as possible, offering free membership to those who need it and encouraging parents to bring babies and children with them. There are no mirrors, or fancy apparel for sale.

My neighbour Temi and I attended a hip-hop dance class together where the dance instructor demonstrated the *pop-your-booty squats* and lunges while carrying a toddler on her hip. After class, Temi explained to me what the gym meant to her during one of the most difficult times in her life.

I was indoors most of the time, just shut up from every other person. Everyone tried their best to make things easier but I guess no one can really reach deep down into your soul and just soothe you. It's time that's needed to work its magic. I guess the community gym started at the right time for me. And here I am.

All of us live with good and bad mental health at different times in our life. Depression, in particular, can arrive seemingly out of nowhere. It has been described as being like a black dog, first by classical poet Horace, then, famously, Churchill, owing to the heaviness, stubbornness and seemingly intractable stuck-ness of depression.

On a visit to the Lowry Gallery in Salford, I noticed how many of Lowry's industrial landscapes include skinny, black dogs amidst the hunched stick men and women spilling out of the factories and mines. The dogs may be a visual metaphor for the working class underdog but I suspect they also hint at Lowry's own deep unease in himself and of an existential loneliness.

I too have always had a thing about skinny, black dogs. There used to be a picture hung on the wall at my grandmother's house which I made when I was about five. In it, there was a little girl in a polka-dot skirt kicking her legs wide, joyful. She was standing at an open window, framed by floral curtains. In the drawing, next to the window and the girl, there was a small, black dog. For reasons that would only make sense three decades later, my childhood drawings always featured small, black dogs. They still do. Blurry, scruffy, wee mongrel dugs.

My drawing of the girl and dog at the window had the thick, confident rakes of colour made from permanent markers – the kind of felt-tipped pens that smell really good and are toxic. I remember making the drawing at Gran's kitchen table. She put it in a frame on the wall, next to postcard prints of Matisse, where it stayed for over thirty years.

Looking at it now in my hands, it also seems significant that the window in my drawing is open to the world outside for, even in the depths of winter, I like to sleep with a window open to fresh air. Above the girl, the window and the dog, I wrote *I am happy today* in black marker pen. And I was. Very happy. When I am happy today, now, which isn't every day of course, I feel like the women in Matisse's twin Dance paintings. However, the dance is one of sustained contentment, of being enough, not necessarily the giddy rush of infantile joy.

The pursuit of happiness is a well-known constitutional phrase, found in the United States Declaration of Independence.[6] The inference is that we need a foundation of happiness or wellbeing – the baseline of being content – to realise life and liberty. The correlating, anxious feeling of *not* feeling enough is regarded as systemic amongst my generation, Generation Y, those born 1980–2000. The continuous feeling of being adrift is a personal affliction, and one which I know is common to many. The causes and balms for anxiety, as part of the experience of the right to health, is something that I asked all of the neighbours I interviewed about.

Ritual was a constant theme. For Buddhist nun Ani Rinchen, aged seventy, meditation and prayer are her ritual. She advised me that I need to find acceptance of what is beyond my control.

Mind is our intention. It starts with intention…It's where all the problems are and it's where all the solutions are. Mind is limitless. So prayer is also a manifestation of your mind. It's your intent. It's not some airy-fairy, wishful thinking. It is focused thinking.

Photographing the pigeons on Constitution Street is my own form of active meditation. With their tattooed necks, skinny legs and darts of green plumage illuminating their blackened bodies, the street doves look like old punks to me. I like watching the familiarity of their rhythm, the routine, the pattern. The way the pigeons move in sync to make many individual diamond shapes combine into one large flock reminds me of the tessellation drawings that used to be pinned to maths classroom walls.

I wait and watch for the street lights to change from red to amber then green. Fixed as they are on the present moment, the birds ascend en masse at green without hesitation or doubt. They rise up and away, toward the peaks of the city skyline in the distance. The pigeons swoop south to west then north and east again, always in a clockwise, meditative formation – the beat of their feathers sounding like the tattered rags of prayer flags left to disintegrate on a stormy mountain pass.

The instinctive fight or flight response anxiety induces is exhausting. It is the distracting feeling of something not being quite right.

If, for some, depression is like a black dog, anxiety can feel, to me, like a panicked bird trapped inside my chest. The repeated flap of the bird's wings as it tries to escape being stuck restricts free flow of breath and speech. My self-assured voice can't be heard above the squawks of criticism coming from the bird.

Anxiety is often common in members of Generation Y because of our job insecurities, the high cost of housing, the exposure of social media and perceptions – real or imagined – of having to prove ourselves. I sometimes wonder if the lack of stability, comparative to our parents and grandparents, is why my generation take so many photographs. It is as though we are framing the Instagrammable present in a kind of digital cement. The photographs are a way of saying *hello, I am here too. By the window, in a nice skirt, with my dog. And I look happy today.*

My neighbour Claire, a gestalt therapist, explained to me that anxiety is cumulative, with neural pathways in the brain establishing patterns that repeat the anxious feelings and responses in a looped cycle. Anxiety can further disengage neurons in the prefrontal cortex linked to memory and decision-making. The constant provocation of twenty-four hour media, pinging and flashing on our phone screens, reinforces the patterns. We have so many choices, so many demands on our attention, that we always miss the mark on giving a careful, considered response and are left feeling not quite good enough as a result.

In Auden's poem 'The Age of Anxiety' four characters meet in a down-town-New York bar and seek an escape from the outside world of 1940s wartime chaos. The setting of the neighbourhood bar, the closed shops on the street and the grouping of unlikely companions echoes Edward Hopper's *Nighthawks*, a painting of a diner late at night. Walls of bottle-green glass separate the private from the public, ease from unease, the them and the us. In their different mediums, the painting, the Auden poem and the subsequent Bernstein symphony[7] of the same name, all speak of the anxiety of boundaries – the inside and outside, the personal and political, and the human need to seek out the familiar and soothing amidst change.

So what hope for feeling better in our current age of anxiety? The exposure and shattering potential of the glass walls that anxiety encases us within can be illuminating in a positive way. Understanding anxiety can make us curious about how we want to be more at ease in the world. The ultimate challenge is to harness stillness in the noisy, revolving chaos of change and to release the trapped bird in the chest.

Morven, an artist living on Constitution Street, told me she felt increasingly uneasy at being bombarded by news updates on her phone. She introduced me to the term 'nomophobia', the irrational fear of being without your mobile phone. Repeated digital intrusion made Morven feel so anxious that she set about crafting a ceramic bowl in which to ritually place her mobile phone at the end of the working day. She refers to the bowl as her pearl.

We chatted inside Morven's flat on the first day of snow in March 2018, when Scotland was under a red weather warning for dangerous weather conditions. Morven's ten-year-old daughter was off school and had built a snowman on the front doorstep. Inside, the desk in Morven's home studio was strewn with a blanket of sketches, buttons, felted scraps and lichen-covered twigs. Yet none of this jumble seemed to cause her anxiety. It was the icy news of chaos and clutter from the outside world which made her feel tense and uncomfortable.

Draft legislation at the Scottish Parliament was being debated, legislation that would potentially block legislative consent to The European Union Withdrawal Bill at Westminster – the first time that the Scottish Parliament in devolved Scotland had withheld consent. A political climate of conflict and confusion clouded the land.

On the street in the first week of March, snow fell continuously for four days and then returned a fortnight later. Schools, offices and cafés closed. The street was free of cars. All was muffled and still. Long, spindly icicles, the claws of the so-called 'Beast from the East', hung menacingly from our tenement window ledges. The newly renovated Port O' Leith bar served shots of vodka, freshly chilled by falling shards of ice, and all of us on the street were at the mercy of the natural world and could do nothing to control it.

The snow forced us to stay local as boundaries closed in and the city lay under an icy siege. The street and its surrounds became our known world. Neighbours helped one another shovel snow from tenement steps, children carried sledges under their arms and strangers smiled at one another in the street with an infantile glee as they crunched over fresh powder. Some of us held hands with one another for the first time. We remembered how to play. All of this made me feel good in the moment.

Feeling good long-term is about physical, mental and social well-being.[8] There is no quick cure to anxiety, depression, and most other psychological conditions, because health is not merely the absence of disease or infirmity. It is socially determined by the conditions in which we are born, grow old, and in which we live, work and play alongside one another. A healthy life – physical, mental and social – requires not only the right to healthcare but also to housing, education, nutrition, social support and child welfare.

All of us must be able to access information, services and facilities in hospitals, surgeries and communities where available, regardless of postcode. In a written constitution, we have the opportunity to state clearly that these rights are universal.

It's time to call closing on mental health stigma, hard drinking and not asking for help. On Constitution Street, I experienced the beginnings of change underway in myself and my neighbours. The street is reinventing itself from a place once notorious for addiction and poverty-related ill-health to become a place where we are starting to feel better about ourselves. We are asserting, with growing self-confidence, our right to stay that way. In the language of declarations, we are actively engaged in the pursuit of happiness.

Everyone has the right to freedom of thought, conscience and religion; this right includes freedom to change his religion or belief, and freedom, either alone or in community with others and in public or private, to manifest his religion or belief in teaching, practice, worship and observance.

Article 18, The Universal Declaration of Human Rights

To cultivate compassion and loving kindness for all beings, that's the aspiration. Of course, it's easier said than done but you know, everyone has some natural compassion.

Ani Rinchen Khandro, Nun, Tibetan Buddhist Temple

The Right to Freedom of Religious Belief

A Shout in the Street

The Virgin Mary watches over us all in my tenement building. I notice tourists at the bus stop opposite jerk their thumbs up to the second floor with bleary-eyed disbelief at the apparition, in the form of a small statue, filling the window frame.

My upstairs neighbour Jordan isn't a church-goer, but he is an enthusiastic collector of religious iconography, much to the irritation of his flatmate. I can feel the manifestation of the lifelike blue and white Madonna figurine weighing down upon me, dangerously, as I sit directly beneath her on the steps outside, sipping a coffee and contemplating matters spiritual. *Oh but what a way to go!* quips Jordan.

Divine intervention for some and a decorative quirk for others, paying attention to the plaster figurine of the Virgin Mary has become a part of the sacred in my everyday. Indeed, much of the tarmac and paving slabs on which we walk is officially designated sacred ground because of the many burials that lie beneath in the old graveyard of South Leith Parish Church, formerly called St Mary's.

There's something about Mary, or Marys, on Constitution Street. Mary of Guise was a member of the old St Mary's congregation. She held court in her native French on nearby Parliament Street and her daughter, Mary Queen of Scots, is believed to have visited the church. The Marys were at the centre of a constitutional crisis in their own age of anxiety. Religious fundamentalism is nothing new. The events of summer 1560 on Constitution Street still shape national and global politics and offer up a reminder of the importance of freedom of belief in a written constitution.

On Easter Sunday, 14 April 1560, the South Leith congregation were assembled for High Mass inside St Mary's. Immediately before the elevation of the Host, a cannonball was shot through the east window, passing directly over the altar, by besieging English Protestant troops. Remarkably, nobody was killed but the continuous bombardment that followed left the church and much of the street in ruins. The mounds of tussocky grass in Leith Links still known locally as Giant's Brae and Lady Fyfe's Brae may be mere hillocks or they may, in fact, be the remains of English staging posts from the 1560 Siege of Leith.

Following its break with Rome, England fought to drive out the Catholic French with help from Scottish Reformation Lords and frequent skirmishes occurred between the two armies. Later romanticised as the 'Rough Wooing' by Sir Walter Scott in the nineteenth century, King Henry VIII's failed attempts to secure an arranged marriage between his heir apparent, Edward, and the infant Mary Queen of Scots stoked violent, sectarian division and suspicion that would not end well for the ill-fated Mary. Leith and, in particular, the land that would later become known as Constitution Street, was at the centre of this religious battlefield.

In 1544, when the Scottish Parliament renounced the tentative agreement for Queen Mary to marry Edward, Henry VIII ordered the complete burning of Edinburgh and the capture of all vessels and loot at Leith harbour in retaliation. Referred to in Scots as closets, the low-level shack housing of local people in Leith was raised to the ground.[1]

At the time of the later English siege in the spring of 1560, Leith was defended by French troops under the authority of Regent Protector

Mary of Guise; her infant daughter Mary Queen of Scots being kept in France for her own protection. Mary of Guise fell ill from heart disease and despite the efforts of her messengers dressed in disguise, she was unable to get the medicines she needed from an apothecary on Leith Walk because of the siege. A black market in prescription medicines was as thriving then as now. She died on 11 June 1560 and The Treaty of Leith/Edinburgh was agreed inside the church on Constitution Street on 5 July 1560, thereby removing both French and English troops from Scotland and leaving Protestant Lords in control of Scotland with a tolerated Catholic monarch, Mary Queen of Scots, on the throne.

The first reformed service of the new Calvinist Kirk was held amidst the rubble and wreckage of the old order. The new South Leith Parish Minister, David Lindsey, later presided over the marriage of Mary's son, King James VI, and Princess Anne of Denmark in Oslo in 1589 after the Princess' fleet was driven by gales to the Norwegian shore. King James VI believed that a coven of witches along the Forth coast had used black arts to try to drown him and his new wife at sea. Under his instruction, the North Berwick Witch Trials unleashed a frenzy of witch hunting in Scotland. Leith women were burned alive for allegedly using cats to summon dark spirits. It is from these real-life stories of torture and women-hating, that the Halloween costume of pointy hat, black cat and broomstick originates.

This persecution of women in the 1590s was misogyny cloaked in the veil of authority – authority like that enjoyed by radical preacher John Knox. He was also a personal friend of the Rev Lindsey of Leith. Both Knox and Mary Queen of Scots are believed to have earlier played golf on Leith Links, the park next to Constitution Street, although not together and not on the Sabbath.

Here and now on Constitution Street, freedom of religious belief is practised in a multi-faith community. The street has four churches still standing, of which two remain in use for religious worship. South Leith Parish Church is Protestant Church of Scotland and St Mary's Star of the Sea belongs to a Catholic order called the Oblates of Mary Immaculate. Then, within the various tributaries leading to Constitution Street, there is a Tibetan Buddhist Temple, a Hindu Mandir, a Mosque and a Sikh Gurdwara.

I invited all of the neighbours I interviewed up and down the street to provide anonymised, written responses to open questions regarding protected characteristics under current equalities law. In response to the question 'How would you describe your religious affiliation, if any?', roughly 60% of the neighbours I met with said that they identified as atheist or agnostic. There was a mix of Protestant, Catholic, Hindu, Muslim, Alevis Muslim and Buddhist responses. And then there were others losing and finding their religion in their own particular ways, including:

I believe in a god but am not quite full Catholic
I hate all the fuckers
Nane! It's aw mental illness
Hindu (but just because my dad would disown me if I put down anything else)
Nature is my religion

To Love Thy Neighbour is a central tenet in nearly all of the main faiths and moral codes. The different religious leaders that I had conversations with shared their own interpretations. Buddhist nun, Ani Rinchen Khandro, explained loving thy neighbour to mean unconditional compassion to all sentient beings and to be about setting patterns of positivity in karmic motion.

It's little things…setting up a pattern of care and responsibility and looking out for other people. But why stop at your neighbour? That's not anywhere written but neighbour to me suggests just the people most around you…the Buddhist view is to accommodate all people, whether you like them or not.

For Rev Iain May, Minister of South Leith Church, loving thy neighbour is fundamentally about forgiveness.

You might not like your neighbour at times, but you have to love them. And it's unconditional, love. If you dig down into things like love, you have to forgive. Once, or as Jesus says, seventy times. But forgiveness and the love, saying you love someone, is just the start…then you have to get back to considering how to rebuild or rekindle the relationship you had before… you have to let go of something, and that could be power or control, or it could just be stubbornness.

While I am familiar with the basic premise of treating others as you wish to be treated, I explained to Iain that, in truth, there are some neighbours that I don't particularly like because of our minor disagreements about noise, passive smoking, common repairs and so on. I was apprehensive about how to open up conversation with those neighbours.

Sometimes conflict just has to be there, it's just a part of it and it might not always be the perfect relationship but you will be able to work together and see it from their perspective… Even Ministers sometimes get it wrong. I know that's very hard to believe!

Learning to let go of the heaviness of personal grievances is perhaps a lifetime's work in progress but through our cultures of encounter on this street and others, nothing ever stays the same in any relationship. There is constant flow. Here on the street, our feet must do the work step by step, crossing over the road. 'Cultures of encounter' is an expression attributed to Pope Francis when he was Archbishop of Buenos Aires.

Behind St Mary's Star of the Sea Church at no. 106 Constitution Street, Christ the Redeemer of Leith (my name), stands with alabaster arms stretched wide. Right fingertips encounter the street to the west with its tower block and the left fingertips reach to the east and the docks. This St Mary's Sacred Heart statue (the official name) caught me in my tracks when I chatted to Pastoral Associate, Sally Fraser.

My colleague, the youth worker, gets really upset about the moss on the statue. I always say, 'look, he's been bearing our sins for 2000 years, I think he can cope with a bit of moss!'

St Mary's Star of the Sea was designed in 1854 by the same architect as the Palace of Westminster, Augustus Pugin. At the time, the Irish immigrant population of Leith numbered about 2,000, with Hibernian Football Club established in 1875. However, Scotland remained deeply divided along sectarian lines into the twentieth century and anti-Irish prejudice was common. A neighbour told me that his best friend from primary school lived in the oldest house on Constitution Street, no. 132a, a somewhat sloping, lopsided house that likely predates the 1790 layout of the street and is the subject of a planning application for a new hotel. The house can be seen in maps from 1794 where very little else still standing is visible. A playground rumour was that the boy's grandfather, whom he lived with, was arrested on charges of gun-running for the IRA and storing weapons at number 132a.

Today, the frame of St Mary's Star of the Sea is tucked away behind a bus shelter and a recruitment agency but, once inside, the nave of the Church expands to be deceptively cavernous and is entered through a candlelit grotto. Once with five separate confession booths, only one remains now, lit by a soft, red glow. The other booths are used as storage rooms. So while Jesus may indeed have been bearing our sins for 2000 years, the reduction in the number of confession booths inside St Mary's might mean that Leithers are sinning less than in the past. *I think people maybe confess in different ways*, suggested Sally as she crossed herself.

> *They maybe make appointments to come and talk to people. But [the confession booths are] quite strange places… There's five of them, yeah, but just one that's in use now. I can't stand it on a Saturday because there's no queuing system and I always feel like they should have something like in Lidl, you know with like tickets… 'sinner number five please!'… That kind of thing. But it doesn't work like that [sighs].*

Sally converted to Catholicism as a student and later took up employment with St Mary's in a pastoral and administrative role. She acknowledged that many of us are fair-weather attenders for key events like communions, confirmations, marriages and Easter Sunday. However, the Constitution Street church has a regular congregation of over 300.

There has always been a diverse and international mix of worshippers at St Mary's, given the Church's proximity to the sea and the flow of visiting sailors from around the world. Inscribed onto the wall of Constitution Street are the words 'keep all seafarers in your prayers.' The Port Chaplaincy from the combined network of Leith churches still goes aboard cargo and cruise ships which visit the docks, to offer worship to sailors from as far away as Indonesia and the Philippines.

At St Mary's, priests live on site at an adjacent Priests' house where the communal rooms contain a snooker table and TV. I guessed that Sally and I are about the same age and I scanned the DVD collection on the shelves in search of *Father Ted*.[2] However, Sally is clearly no Mrs Doyle. Throughout my time paying close attention to constitutional change, I frequently bumped into her on the street. I particularly enjoyed Sally's contemporary 'Reply from the Lassies' at the Leith Dockers Club Burns Supper in January 2018, where she managed to include the words feminist and vagina in verse, which she sung unaccompanied to a packed-out hall of retired dockers and their wives.

Rev. Iain May of South Leith Parish also practises what he preaches. He signs off his emails to me with *Blessings*. Taking up his calling to the Ministry in 2012, Iain, a former naval officer and commercial banker, was troubled by the concentration of pawn brokers, cash-for-gold and payday-loan companies surrounding Constitution Street. Drawing upon his past life as a banker, he helped set up the Castle Community Bank. While regulated as a credit union, the bank has no shareholders and, instead, is fully owned by its members who vow to invest surplus funds into local communities. Whereas a foodbank is there to help feed people, the community bank exists to support financial health.

About six months after I started in the parish, I was walking through the local shopping area and counted nine payday lenders or cash converters within literally a couple of hundred yards. There's cash-a-cheque, a broker's, loan sharks. And people feel it's their only choice. So we have to provide different choices.

In the Cleansing of the Temple story in the Bible, Jesus overthrew the tables of the money changers and cast them out from the house of prayer. The corrupting power of money is a familiar thread in other faiths too.

Ani Rinchen Khandro, told me the story of how a Tibetan Buddhist Temple came to be at home in the former Bank of Leith building. She had been tasked with finding a new property for the Edinburgh branch of Samye Ling and immediately knew that there was something special about the dome-shaped building next to Constitution Street.

> *It's oval-shaped with a big dome and it looked really like what we would call in Buddhism a mandala. A mandala is like a sacred drawing.*

After the usual negotiations with estate agents and mortgage providers, the sale went ahead. She had been worried about entering into competition with another bidder but then she found out that the rival bidder was a global coffee chain.

> *[I thought] oh let's just go for it. And in retrospect, now that I know Leith a bit more, the Leith people and whole ethos of the place is very independent and so I don't think they would have accepted a Starbucks. We [Leithers] are very independent, or interdependent, I should say, in the Buddhist way of saying things.*

The Leith Banking Company Leith was established in 1793 when Leith was at the height of its merchant prosperity. My own ancestor born in 1801, Captain James Smith, was most likely a customer at the Bank of Leith in his later, wealthier years and Sir Walter Scott is known to have also been a customer.

Today's goings on inside the former temple to mammon include regular guided meditation, and yoga workshops. It was the signature Buddhist string of prayer flags fluttering outside that first caught my attention when walking along the street. I knocked on the door to enquire about yoga classes and Ani greeted me with a welcoming, homely smile. Such is the karmic flow of community, connection and coincidence, that we realised we had met before on Holy Isle off the coast of Arran in the late 1990s and also, quite possibly, at the main Samye Ling Buddhist centre in Eskdalemuir, Dumfriesshire, where Ani first found her faith.

I used to have hair as long as you! she laughed, slipping into her Mancunian accent. Ani (Buddhist for nun and meaning precious) stood in the doorway to the Temple, dressed in her maroon and saffron-coloured robes with an additional fleece and scarf wrapped around her. *I'm being a bit of a woose today. It's so cold!*

Ani Rinchen's long blonde locks were shaved off fifteen years ago when she vowed to leave behind her former life as Jackie Glass, but there's still a glimmer of the fashion model and 1960s socialite she once was. In the middle of our conversation, Ani apologised for having to pause to take a phone call, during which I heard her speak the French she picked up while modelling in Morocco. A former girlfriend of footballer George Best, she moved from Manchester to the London of the swinging sixties, during a time of political and social rebellion, but soon became disillusioned with the hedonistic lifestyle.

Describing herself as being *as old as India herself* (seventy, at the time of our conversation) and like many Tibetan Buddhists in the west, Ani did not grow up with the Buddhist faith. Raised by Jewish and Catholic parents, she was agnostic until travelling in southeast Asia and reading books by the Dalai Lama inspired her to explore spirituality more deeply. The turning point for committing to Buddhism was hearing His Holiness give a talk in Scotland entitled 'Inner Peace leads to World Peace.' She had driven up from Manchester during a snowstorm to hear him speak.

*I'd travelled around the world and had met many kinds of people…I was
a little bit sceptical but for the first time in my life I thought, 'Wow, I want
some of what you've got!'*

While she is now *kind of at home* in Leith, her hometown is Manchester
and she described to me the emotional tug of wanting to be back
there when news reached her of the bombing at Manchester Arena in
May 2017. Sadness was mixed with an intense pride at how her fellow
Mancunians responded to the terror attack with compassion and loving
kindness. She was inspired to write a poem in tribute to Manchester,
about home, faith and the city's pithy street wit.

In our conversation about pithy street wit, Ani explained that, for her,
the meaning of life is rubbing along with all different types of people.
To find happiness, she said, we need to get to the root of suffering.
Acceptance of the human condition, its flaws and its abundant capacity
to love and forgive, was a recurring theme in all my conversations with
faith leaders and neighbours on Constitution Street.

Most national constitutions have a religious overtone and I began to
wonder if organised religion itself is a form of social contract, a constitution of sorts. For example, is the commandment of the Old Testament
and the Torah *Thou Shalt Not Kill* and the Koranic values of justice and
mercy primarily constitutional laws to keep peace in community during
the context in which they were written? Rev Iain May interprets the
old texts for our own day and age. He told me that he doesn't want the
Church to be seen *as some ecclesiastical cult, a wee secret society*.

Once the largest parish church in Scotland, a thousand people each
week still pass through the South Leith Parish Church hall with its
community café, Girl Guides, line-dancing and parent-and-toddler
groups. Along with Iain, I attended my first public meeting of the Scottish

independence referendum campaign in the church hall in 2013. It was a dreich November night but the queue to enter snaked along the street in single file.

The church has been a landmark at the centre of constitutional debate for centuries. Sitting discussing ecumenical matters inside the vestry, Iain wasn't joking when he acknowledged to me the heavy burden of history he feels weighing upon his shoulders. Officially founded in 1483 and noted to have been twice the length of the present kirk (comparable to St Giles in the Old Town of Edinburgh), the Church in the Midst is mentioned in earlier Scottish court records. During the Cromwellian period, the church was a meeting place between covenanters and royalists in an attempt to reach a peaceful compromise and avoid war. The diplomatic attempts failed and the church was used as a munitions store, a *magasin*, for Oliver Cromwell's troops during the resulting six-year conflict. Cromwell's army built a fort in nearby North Leith which is now home to the Citadel Youth Centre.

Now, alongside the familiar decor of a Parish church – Sunday School quilts depicting the four seasons in felt, war memorial plaques and a registrar of christenings – there are several royal coats of arms positioned beneath the hammerbeam roof: Mary of Guise, Mary Queen of Scots, James VI of Scotland (I of England) and Charles I. Here is the only place in Scotland where four consecutive coats of arms of a royal house can be seen. Providing spiritual guidance in such a setting is not a job for the faint-hearted.

> *I couldn't do this job if it was just a job. I would be mad. And so would my family. They wouldn't put up with it. And neither would I because I would never see them.*

Iain acknowledged that more than any welcome, it is often rejection that people remember when they encounter religion. Throughout history, it has been suppression of the right to freedom of belief that has put up walls between different faiths and communities. In the era of Trump, the building and paying for of walls has come to further symbolise segregation and suspicion of 'the other'. When the 1790 layout of Constitution Street was completed, the grounds of South Leith Parish Church were reduced and a walled garden was offered by city authorities in compensation.

Today's Church in the Midst is enclosed in between Constitution Street and the Kirkgate shops. Among the many Edinburgh Tram project controversies in recent years, the bringing down of this wall to allow for the broadening of the road and the fixture of tram cables was one of the most divisive for my neighbours. To my surprise, Iain is in favour of tearing down the Church wall.

> *The wall that comes down Constitution Street hides this church. There's been a site here for over a thousand years so [the wall is] not that old really. It was all open back then, it was like a field. So it would be nice to open it up again.*

One day – we can't be sure when – the sea will take back the silt and sand on Constitution Street. Sea levels are rising globally. In 2017–2018 on Constitution Street, we experienced both heat waves and cold snaps, more extreme than any I had ever known. Our feet therefore do the work of encounter on borrowed ground and time. Energy spent constructing fences and walls here or across national borders elsewhere is wasted while we remain both citizens of nowhere[3] and everywhere.

In the first week of December 2017, President Trump declared a shift in US foreign policy by recognising the religiously divided city of

Jerusalem to be the capital city of Israel, thereby igniting further anger across the Holy Land. Meanwhile, those of all faiths and none stood freezing together at the top of Constitution Street on a stormy, late afternoon for the Leith Christmas carol concert.

Somewhat straggly and with a handful of fairy lights making it look like a fishing net had been flung across it, the Christmas tree propped up next to Queen Victoria was no Germanic prince. I overheard someone in the crowd scoff, *Here, that was the tree that Stockbridge [a wealthier part of Edinburgh] got last year. The Cooncil must have stuck it in the freezer and geein it tae us! The cheek o' it!*

I recognised many neighbours in the crowd. Bedecked in her regal coat of leopard print and with tinsel in her hair, Mary, Queen of Leith, was instantly recognisable as she handed out carol sheets. The assembled Leithers of wise men and women mumbled a rendition of 'Come All Ye Faithful' before the primary school choir in Santa hats took to a makeshift stage. The microphone for the official dignitaries opening the concert had been turned on prematurely and we were treated to the children's own commentary on the Leith nativity broadcast at loud volume. A little girl in unicorn pyjamas complained to her mother, *Mummy, why wasn't I allowed to be in the choir?* while another clyped to a teacher, *That boy's picking his nose!*

A semblance of order was restored by the teachers in charge and neighbours wished one another season's greetings before pushing on through the gusts of a storm and the dark of 4pm in December. Unusually for early winter by the sea, the Water of Leith river was frozen over and I watched tiny sparrows tiptoe across its glassy surface. Some neighbours said it was the coldest winter since 1970 and wrapped cling film onto their window panes as makeshift double-glazing. Outside the Port O' Leith bar, another neighbour proudly showed off her Rudolph onesie costume to the pub congregation in preparation for party season. She is a tall woman, so the pelt of reindeer polyester came to a stop mid-white shin.

Back in church the next day, Rev Iain May continued his tour of the many historical details. We paused in sombre contemplation at the First World War memorial. My eyes immediately focused in on the cluster of surnames close to my own in the alphabet, the many Mackenzies, Napiers, Nesbits. Lost brothers, fathers, sons, cousins, friends and neighbours of the street. In addition to the hundreds of Leith men and boys killed in the prime of their youth during battle, Britain's worst rail disaster involved around 500 men of the Leith Battalion of The Royal Scots heading to Liverpool to set sail for Gallipoli, Turkey in 1915. More than 200 soldiers and twelve civilians were killed and a further 246 people were injured.

Contemporary reports of the incident were covered up by government censors for fear it would damage the nation's wartime spirit, but the day after the crash 107 coffins were returned from the disaster to Leith in a procession lined with more than 3,000 local people on Constitution Street. One hundred years later in 2015, it was Iain who led the anniversary commemorations. His great uncle died in the crash.

Iain and I faced the memorial plaque inside the church in a solemn silence for some time and then Iain continued to read aloud a list of surnames. He paused and winked at me, checking to notice if I had spotted a link to more recent times. *Renton. Perhaps even a... Mark Renton?* A fine Leith name to choose.[4]

Ach, Jemma, we're only human! Iain joked as he shrugged his shoulders and waved me off from the house of God, back onto the icy street pavement outside. In the distance, I could hear a busker in the Kirkgate shopping precinct gently strumming the chords to Jeff Buckley's version of 'Hallelujah'. And like this, the interplay between light and dark, in between hope and despair, in between losing and finding our beliefs, continued its perpetual flow.

On Christmas Eve, I walked to the Watchnight Service under a moonlit sky with my neighbour from across the road. We pushed our way through the many layers of history inside the church. Bundled-up neighbours sat in coats and hats sharing an uncomfortable pew. All of us the most unlikely of church-goers. After the customary hymns and prayers, we listened to Iain's words from the pulpit about a family from Nazareth who had searched for room at an inn. The message about refuge and safety in an age of mass migration and homelessness was less than subtle. He concluded by asking in the paternalistic, sarcastic tone only Scots can perfect with any warmth: *Well then, Merry Christmas…Have you lot not got homes to get to now? Away with you all!* And we did. Get away home and say goodnight. Via the many inns on the street.

Writing about the streets of Dublin, James Joyce said that he was able to get to the heart of all the cities of the world because in the particular was contained the universal.[5] That all relationships conclude is one of life's few universal certainties. Expecting anything different is part of our human suffering. For those of us not of religious faith, we at least live on through our conversations. Our shouts in the street. Our good karma, if that's your thing. Being *only human* brims over with all the consciousness of our interconnection. Attendance at church services may have declined in modern Scotland but I witnessed that people still retain a deep, personal faith. A written constitution needs to be a broad church respecting the rights of people of all different forms of belief and none. We have to keep on paying attention to the sacred in the everyday here and now, on Constitution Street, with all of our worldly compassion and kindness. I believe that we're already doing it.

Everyone has the right to work, to free choice of employment, to just and favourable conditions of work and to protection against unemployment...

Article 23, The Universal Declaration of Human Rights

It's a blessing to do a job that you feel strongly about rather than having to sell something you don't agree with.

Sally, Pastoral Associate, 106 Constitution Street

The Right to Work

Flitting from Port to Port

Early one winter morning, Storm Caroline whipped through the Northern Hemisphere, leaving a trail of destruction and debris in its wake. Former docker and window cleaner Dougie, could be seen from the street below leaping from one window ledge of my tenement building to the next without a ladder or harness.

I've shared many an early morning cup of coffee with Dougie over the past decade as he wipes away a month's worth of muck and stoor from my windows to let the light find its way back inside. In the fermenting dawn when his customers are finishing their breakfasts and hurriedly readying themselves for a day of work in the outside world, a window cleaner has insights and reflections into the most intimate aspects of our domestic lives. In his work, he sees us as we are, at home.

Oh the stories I could tell you about the folk on this street!

Dougie's first job was as an apprentice pipefitter at Leith Docks. In his younger years, he drank in a pub called Dirty Windaes, since converted into flats. Now with an established window cleaning business, he likes the early starts and has gained a reputation for high-rise acrobatics, once having been mistaken for a Fringe performer during August in Edinburgh.

There was no health and safety back then at the docks of course. All the young boys were just in their trainers. A lad died falling from a boat. I was

on a shift that day and we just had to keep on working. And you used to
be able to just walk around anywhere you wanted. Not now though.

On the street today, Workingrite, a social enterprise and charity, delivers
work-based mentoring and education for young people aged sixteen to
eighteen. Setting up Workingrite in 2004 in response to high unemployment and educational underachievement in the Leith area, my neighbour
Sandy had the goal of matching young people in work experience placements with older role models. Sandy's own journey was one of manual
labour when he left school, followed by trade union activity and latterly
consultancy.

It takes longer for some young people to find the right path, and there is
absolutely nothing wrong with that. Far from it. Taking longer is probably
the best decision they could make.

Two thirds of young people on Workingrite placements progress to a
job, apprenticeship or further learning, but Sandy told me that youth
unemployment in the Leith area is still higher than the city and national
averages.[1]

In many languages, the verbs to do and to make are the same. Indeed,
in Scotland, we call our poet laureate the Makar. Often the first question
that comes up on meeting someone for the first time is 'and what do you
do?' The doing referring to our chosen path – how we earn *a living*. Few
people are lucky enough to do a job they love so much that they want its
title to define them, and the question is particularly reductive for those out
of formal work for a myriad of reasons such as unemployment, disability,
illness or retirement. Then there are those, predominantly women, whose
'doing' is to care for others – children, ageing parents or partners with

support needs — a whole sector of the workforce whose activity isn't recorded by GDP measurements of economic growth. This is despite the word economy coming from the Greek *ecos* meaning household.

I made the mistake of asking my neighbours about what they *do*. When I asked them to tell me their occupation, many prefaced their response with detail about their creative lives at home. Sometimes, it felt like this came up because it was such an important part of them being known and valued. The act of making appeared intrinsically linked to self-worth and interaction with one another. At other times, the tone was more of a justification or rationale for lacking a clearly defined job title, being unemployed, being wealthy and not having to work full-time, or having a portfolio of work interests. In all ways, the making and the doing that I heard about seemed to centre on perceptions of being good enough. Having enough. Doing enough.

A better opening question to a neighbour was, 'How did you get here?' I learnt that the stories of how we came to work on Constitution Street are the stories of heavy industries being replaced by creative industries, of adaptability through adversity, migration routes, the links between North East Scotland and the South Pole, and of a secret beach hidden on the outer perimeter of the docks.

Mechanic Donald came to Constitution Street looking for a workshop in which to repair old 2CV cars. He set up business in the yard that was previously used as a cooperage for Whyte and Mackay whisky and then wire basket-making. The tenement overlooking this yard once belonged to the Lord Provost of Leith and housed a masonic lodge. The historical setting also caught the attention of film producers and the yard features in the film *Jude* starring Kate Winslet.[2] Dressed in his trademark red overalls and lumberjack hat, Donald was in a reflective mood when we chatted.

He told me that he thinks he will retire when sections of the street likely close for the Edinburgh Trams extension, and so is considering the *how* of his leaving work.

The how-do-you-do of our work lives is also something that my neighbour Paul gave me new insights into. I first met Paul through his training sessions with disabled access charity, Euan's Guide, based at 29 Constitution Street. Paul has lived and worked on or near the street for twenty years.

> *For me as a disabled person, as a wheelchair user, powerchair user specif-*
> *ically, I'm always watching how the street changes to become more useful*
> *to me, or perhaps accepting of me. As it is today, it's really good because*
> *the pavements have good surfaces, good textures with drop kerbs, and there*
> *are controlled crossings. It's actually one of the better streets. But I'm still*
> *always on the lookout. Always alert, expecting something. I like it at a*
> *weekend when the street is not so busy and I can get more of a sense of the*
> *street's architecture and go, 'Wow, that was the day when Leith was really*
> *somewhere!'*

Back in the day when Leith was the busiest port in Scotland, the docks at the end of Constitution Street were a thriving market place of raw goods imported, exported and manufactured. Famous ships that set sail from the port included the 1698 ill-fated Darien expedition by the old Kingdom of Scotland to present day Panama in the Gulf of Darien. The failed attempt to establish a Scottish colony called Caledonia contributed to the near-bankruptcy of Scotland and eventual Treaty of Union with England and Wales in 1707. Along the further lanes, wynds and riverbank by the street there was ship-building, cement-making, leather manufacture, rope, twine- and sail-making. Then coopering, tanning, glass-making, soap-making, juice-making, vinegar-making and biscuit-making. Walking along Constitution Street in the eighteenth, nineteenth and early twentieth century would have been an assault on the eyes, nose and ears.

My neighbour Iain grew up on the street in the 1950s and told me that his father worked for Christian Salvesen whalers. Salvesens were the biggest whaling company in the world and had their offices to the east of Constitution Street.

Whaling dominated working life in Leith for 300 years. In the early eighteenth century a boiling house was established at Timberbush. Later owned by the Wood family, the pungent, oily stench of boiling blubber was known locally as Woods' scent bottle.[3]

The Edinburgh Whale Fishing Company had its first ship, *The Trial*, equipped for an expedition to Greenland in 1750 but the earliest records of whaling from Leith date from 1615 when crews hunted for whales in the North Sea. Thereafter, there were annual sailings to Greenland departing each April from Leith and returning in the summer months. In the twentieth century, whaling fleets switched to South Georgia. Salvesen's whaling ships also transported live penguins from South Georgia back to Edinburgh Zoo, making Edinburgh the first zoo in the world to house and breed penguins.

New Leith Harbour, also known as Port Leith, was a whaling station on the northeast coast of South Georgia established in 1909 and finally abandoned in 1965. It is now off-limits to visitors due to high levels of asbestos and falling masonry but, at its peak, in the early twentieth century new Leith Harbour stationed 500 men and was the biggest whaling station in the world. A steam-saw in the bone loft was used for cutting up the skulls and spines of whales which were then boiled to extract oil. Up to twenty-nine tonnes of oil could be extracted from each whale by putting its blubber, meat and bone through different industrial processes.

In 1933, a third of the fat in British margarines came from whales. Port Leith was also the whaling station that Ernest Shackleton and his men walked into after their epic escape from Antarctica and journey across South Georgia. According to Iain:

> *Until the 1950s, many a young Leither was able to finance his marriage from the money he could make on a whaling trip to South Georgia where he worked hard, earned good wages and had little opportunity for spending what he earned.*

I remember watching *How to Save the World*,[4] a documentary about the origins of Greenpeace and the internal power struggles and ethical dilemmas faced by its founding members. My friend and I had winced and looked down at the carpeted dark of the cinema, away from the grotesque panorama filling the screen with seal pups and whales being sliced up by harpoons and clubs. The ocean fizzed a furious red.

I grew up in Dundee, a former industrial port city. Dundee, like Leith, sweated through the grime and the heat of nineteenth century industrialisation thanks in part to its role in amassing crew members for whaling voyages to the Arctic and Antarctica and for processing the whale carcasses into meat, oil and bone when the ships returned. Street names like East Whale Lane, Baltic Street and Candlemaker Row lay bare the recent butchery of highly intelligent, sociable marine mammals. Whaling helped people from poverty-stricken Scotland survive.

In April 2016, I travelled to Greenland with artists from across the western Nordic region – the Faroe Islands, Iceland, Denmark, Orkney and Shetland – for a study visit to learn about how the creativity of people in sparsely populated, rural communities – places and people at the edge of the sea. I had felt my own edges too and hoped, in vain, to catch a glimpse of a live whale in the sea.

On the flight from Reykjavik, Iceland, to Kulusuk, Eastern Greenland, and then onto Tasiilaq by small helicopter, great expanses of shape-shifting ice, sea, and mountains had unfurled below – a landscape both utterly beautiful and terrifying in its duality of geological strength and vulnerability to change. Chunks of menacing iceberg lazily slipped and slid into the sea like cubes popped from a rubber tray, deliciously clinking against the side of a pint glass on a summer's day. Then when the sun set and night-time temperatures plummeted, the ice cubes reformed anew into a solid, elemental state back in the living, polar freezer.

Seeing the Arctic world from above, it became clear to me that humans, the best survivors of all, inhabit a vast blue planet, and must, too, have emerged from the sea. As Scottish naturalist and explorer, John Muir, wrote: 'When we try to pick out anything by itself, we find it hitched to everything else in the Universe.'[5] Everything and everyone is interconnected. An ice-world, as I experienced briefly in Greenland, is a world without trees, a world where leaves never brush against bare arms, where the drip, drip sound of thawing ice in April reverberates across the fjords and where men from North-East Scotland risked their lives on the high seas to bring home a decent working wage for their families.

After near oblivion, global whale populations have started to recover. A Salvesen harpoon anchored into the concrete along the Leith Shore, next to picnic benches and canal barges, is a gory reminder of our conflicted relationship with the natural world. Above the doors of the former Salvesen offices there is still a large bust of Poseidon, god of the sea, but the building is now a Chinese restaurant.

This far-easterly section of Constitution Street was a hub of heavy industry connected to the sea before a steep rise in unemployment in the 1980s. Making new out of old is still the day-to-day work of some businesses next to the docks. Daltons scrap yard on the street has been run by Joe Dalton since the 1960s.

> *Scrap Yards are called bad neighbours but that's a bit harsh. Nowadays we try to close up at four-thirty so that people can come home and have their tea in peace, read a book or watch the telly.*

The main customers at Daltons used to be printers, shipyards, breweries, distilleries and foundries. Joe is confident that Daltons has a future on the street but nowadays regular customers to the family business are sole traders like plumbers and electricians or passing members of the antiques trade looking to pick up a pair of brass candlesticks. It's no longer cash-in-hand and customers must provide proof of identity to guard against the frequent theft of lead and copper piping.

Daltons' immediate neighbour is the Creative Exchange co-working space that hosts web designers, photographers and marketing consultants. Collectively, creative industries in Scotland contribute £4.6 billion to the economy annually, which is more than the extractive industries of oil and gas.[6] The cheaper commercial rents in Leith combined with economic development grants have made the area a growing hub for start-up businesses, in contrast to the heavy manufacturing of the past.

I don't have to speculate at the occupations of our past neighbours from history because only three years after Constitution Street was built, *Williams Directory 1793* formally recorded all the official occupations in Edinburgh.[7]

Most registered occupations were makers or merchants of one kind or another and workers in the same trade often lived in the same district of the town. For example, the shoemakers, or cordiners, all lived at the southern end of the Leith Parish. There were nine trade incorporations in total, acting together as a kind of federation and known collectively as the Traders – coopers, tailors, fleshers, weavers, baxters (bakers), cordiners, hammermen, wrights (carpenters) and barbers. There was also a wig-maker recorded on Constitution Street in 1793.

Today's mix of businesses on the street doesn't include a wig-maker but there is a puppet-maker. My neighbour Mari produces over a thousand puppets each year from her front room on Constitution Street. Her clients at Picture to Puppet include TV production companies, publishers, ventriloquists, counsellors, child psychologists, speech therapists and nursery schools. She told me that she tries not to get too attached to the hand-stitched creations but admits to liking it when customers send her updates from the puppets' new homes. Her favourite commissions are those where she is asked to design and make a puppet directly from a child's drawing and she also offers a teddy bear stitch-up surgery.

I chatted to Mari in the week before Christmas as she and her studio assistant attached plaits of woollen hair to the heads of fortune-teller dolls ready to be dispatched around the world. Propped up in the street-facing windows of her ground floor tenement flat there was also a 3ft-tall purple dragon puppet, a giraffe, a moose, and a fat man in a suit with straw-yellow, woollen hair. In the year of the #MeToo campaign, Donald Trump puppets, pin cushions and voodoo dolls were Mari's bestsellers at Christmas.

Nearly all entries in the list of occupations from 1793, including the wig-makers, were for men. Only a handful of women were noted as proprietors of lodging houses or pubs. The informal economy of caring, cleaning, domestic servitude and prostitution was unrecorded.

In considering our right to work, it would be remiss not to touch upon the oldest form of street work – prostitution. Like all ports, sex work has always been present in and around the Constitution Street area.

Unsurprisingly, it's a difficult subject to get people with first-hand experience to talk about. The police told me that street prostitutes have moved away from Constitution Street and now solicit in the aptly named John's Place next to Leith Links.

The relative merits of legalising or criminalising the industry and/or the men who buy sex remains a deeply divisive issue on the street. Street prostitution today is confined to set areas under the support of the police and women's aid charities and so is largely tolerated by local residents.

Local resident and SNP councillor Rob, recalled it being a different story in the 1980s:

> *Quite a few [sex workers] in those days used to drink in the Port O' Leith bar. They wanted to go somewhere where they could be warm and not be threatened and be themselves. And that was allowed in the Port O' Leith and people seemed, to me anyway, to treat them with respect. I think Mary [the landlady] was always very caring towards them.*

The abusive experiences and tough life choices encountered by women working the streets today should not be confused with Constitution Street's former reputation as a place for *dancing girls* in pubs and clubs. However, I often heard the occupations conflated in my interviews. Perhaps it is because both forms of work strike at the heart of persistent gender imbalances of economic and social power.

The mix is something that people referred to again and again in reflecting on working life past and present. The decline of Scotland's once busiest port is attributed to a combination of factors – the loss of shipbuilding, the port being bought over by a private equity firm, the introduction of containerisation making many manual jobs become mechanised, and the breaking of unions in Thatcherite Britain in the late 1980s. Only a handful of the remaining forty staff based on site at the docks today, including office and engineering staff, now live locally.

Two thirds of goods entering or leaving the European mainland are still transported by sea but shipping regulations following the September 2001 terror attacks in New York mandated the docks' owners, Forth Ports, to increase security. The introduction of high metal fences, barbed wire and twenty-four hour inspection brought about the final dislocation of the port from the street.

The destination boards, giant vehicle hangers and men patrolling in high-visibility jackets now bring to mind a maritime airport at a colonial outpost. It smells of diesel oil and bitumen. Overgrown weeds rustle in the sea breeze and the expanse of surplus industrial land is littered with scrap metal and glass. The message to local residents is clear – keep out.

Ray is Asset Manager for Forth Ports. Members of the public are no longer permitted to walk through the docks so after I had left my passport with reception for security clearance, Ray gave me a tour of the vast site by car. The docks appeared at the end of Constitution Street like an abandoned fairground of sea-lock gates, swing bridges, hangers labelled with numbers painted as tall as their walls and cranes poised like T-rexes with mechanical claws hovering over heaps of junk. I felt like I was experiencing a transient no-man's land suspended between heritage and renewal.

Ray explained that the biggest income now comes from cruise ships berthing in the docks, averaging fifty ships and 20,000 passengers over the course of a year. However, the resulting spending power and job creation from tourism doesn't stay in Leith as the passengers are bussed by coach directly into Edinburgh city centre on arrival.

With the downturn in the oil industry, some commercial vessels have stayed in the port longer than planned. On the day of my tour, several ships were berthed in the dry dock for repair and maintenance. The red and blue primary colours of their hulls jarred against the metallic grey hues of absence pervading the rest of the yard. The stationary ships were branded *Voyager, Pegasus, Apache, Hercules*. All the while, the Filipino crew of one of the vessels shivered up and down the quayside in their naval uniforms.

In the car, Ray and I crossed over iron swing bridges and the railway tracks that transported cargo to the city and we passed the sea wall where scenes in *Trainspotting 2* were filmed. Behind the wall there is a small, hidden stretch of white sandy beach at an outcrop called Black Rocks where grey seals come to sunbathe. Far away from any harpoons and nestled against planks of driftwood and discarded tyres, these seals have a private deck with views across the Forth to Inchmickery island.

Then, surrounding the empty grain silo, I saw hillocks of sand, scrap sheet metal and green, glass bottles ready to be crushed. The equivalent of 33 million wine bottles are recycled at Leith docks each year. Ray explained that landfill tax is considerably less when aggregate is broken down, so the docks is also the place where commercial landmarks come to be dismembered and die. He pointed to one pile of concrete shards and glass that had two weeks previously formed the St James shopping centre in Edinburgh city centre. The whole thing resembled a gory scene of one rusting beast devouring another.

This recycling plain is crisscrossed by the remains of train tracks. They were part of a railway line that transported coal to the docks. The tracks now peter out into clumps of red poppies blooming amidst railway sleepers, broken glass and wilting memories of Leith's industrial heyday.

On first impression, it seems a desolate, ghostly landscape, but look and listen closely and there is a new squad of workers busy in the constantly evolving coastal ecology. Britain's largest colony of common terns, *sterna hirundo*, migrates to the far end of Constitution Street each summer to build their nests atop the floating artificial platforms of the wet docks.

The birds' nests are sometimes little more than a bare scrape in the gravel but are comfortably lined with bits of industrial debris. Also known as a sea swallow, the common tern has silver-grey and white plumage, orange legs and a narrow, red-pointed bill. The murmuration of 900 breeding pairs arrives in the UK each April and flits south again for wintering in the tropics, in search of other flat, poorly vegetated surfaces close to water. The terns have one of the longest migration routes of all birds, with an average round trip of 35,000km each year.[8]

The sea swallows are shy and do not like to be disturbed, preferring to be left alone to eat sandeels. After detailed scientific study of the colony by ornithologists, looking into the impact of the industrial environment on the nesting chick populations, the birds have been given protected status by the establishment of The Imperial Dock Lock Special Protection Area. Thus, all further regeneration of the docks area must now take into account the flight path of these industrious migrants. Just as the humans of Constitution Street once reclaimed the shore for work space, the birds are taking back the sea in strength of numbers. The interconnection of nature that John Muir described as the hitching to everything in the Universe continues.

A future for the port and our working lives in this neighbourhood depends on sustaining a diversity of trades and businesses that will keep people here, as well as just and favourable conditions for us, the workers, in balance with the natural world. As my neighbour Paul said to me:

Constitution Street is a street that goes somewhere. It's a street with purpose. I always think I'm on it because I'm going somewhere. This isn't history. The street is a living entity and is different in different seasons, times of day. Just like us.

Our written constitution should also be a living entity, with the linguistic flexibility and legislative scrutiny to be interpreted for the different times ahead. Much as we no longer work as whalers, wig-makers, or shipbuilders, today's occupations on Constitution Street will be unrecognisable to the workers of the future.

In my interviews about work, and in my own work to sift and analyse the evidence, I learnt that the importance of feeling useful cannot be underestimated. The right to work in The Universal Declaration of Human Rights goes on to state further that 'everyone, without discrimination, has the right to equal pay for equal work' and that this right must include 'an existence worthy of human dignity, and supplemented, if necessary, by other means of social protection.'[9] Our work in caring, volunteering, studying and looking after ourselves and one another are all useful forms of doing that deserve to be better valued in a new Scotland. The work to achieve that attitudinal and economic change must be part of the constitutional conversation.

Everyone has the right to freedom of opinion and expression; this right includes freedom to hold opinions without interference and to seek, receive and impart information and ideas through any media and regardless of frontiers. Everyone has the right freely to participate in the cultural life of the community, to enjoy the arts and to share in scientific advancement and its benefits...

Articles 19 and 27, The Universal Declaration of Human Rights

Music is a conversation really. It's a way of getting all that stuff that goes on in your head out.

Rod, Musician, 100 Constitution Street

The Right to Freedom of Expression

The Making of Us

What relevance has singing, poetry and drawing in the serious matter of drafting a written constitution?

My friend Simon is an Art Therapist. When trying to convince NHS managers of the need for continued investment in therapeutic practice, he sat the managers down in a group and asked each to draw a picture of their family home using coloured pencils and pens. The men and women in suits set about enthusiastically sketching the recognisable rectangles and triangles of a classic house shape, complete with flowers in the garden and family members at the door. Simon then asked each to pass their drawing to the person next to them and, on receiving someone else's drawing, to make it as ugly as possible. Without much need for encouragement, the pretty drawings of houses and gardens were soon defaced with thick, black scribbles, the family faces graffitied or mutilated and some sheets of paper crumpled entirely. The drawings were then returned to the original, somewhat upset, artists. Simon had demonstrated that creative expression goes to the heart of our sense of self and of feeling safe, of being at home. When we create something, we put a piece of ourselves into it. Making matters, because it is a statement of expression and intent.

Freedom of expression and participation in culture are perhaps the most meaningful human rights of all. Here are the rights to tell our own stories and to be all that we can be. Although qualified, not the least by the balancing of others' rights, engaging in expression and cultural life is an enabler to other rights including the right to education.

Mark-making seems to matter all the more if there are others to bear witness to it and to acknowledge the creative effort. I had intended that my street conversations be a type of bearing witness to the realisation of human rights.

Culture, often revealed through our art and our making, is like a long, continuous conversation. It creates the constructed space[1] to say and hear uncomfortable things face to face. I learnt this first-hand in the courtroom when working as a legal intern in The Hague.

The international criminal tribunals set up in the mid 1990s by the United Nations after the Bosnian and Rwandan genocides did not originally include provision for outreach services.[2] Insufficient thought had been given to how the legal process of analysing evidence could be communicated to victims and witnesses who were not legally trained. Highly traumatised people travelled to another country, often for the first time, to give testimony in an international tribunal and weren't always told how their personal accounts did or did not prove legal tests like command responsibility in humanitarian law.

Things had gotten better by the time I was listening to very uncomfortable stories face to face in court. Large screens were assembled in the countries where atrocities had occurred to broadcast proceedings live from court. Pictorial and dramatised summaries of legal process were also developed to explain to children how a courtroom functions or to overcome language barriers. The experience of learning about this inspired me to leave an early career in law in favour of outreach work and nurturing creative participation in myself and others. I wanted to explore how to make the law accessible for the people it exists to serve – the people whose real-life experiences shape case law precedent, not the lawyers and judges who speak to one another in Latin maxims.

I am still learning about how to do this. I do know that in any creative conversation, intrinsic and instrumental, there is a relationship between artist and audience, between a You and a Me. Paying attention to participation in the cultural life of the street, I heard stories about strangers becoming neighbours and lifelong friends. Because, when someone adds to the story you are telling, they become no longer a stranger.

When I met Fi, a gardener and keen knitter of Fairisle jumpers, she extolled the importance of using her hands in self-expression.

It's the hands, isn't it? Get your hands dirty a bit. Because it's touching wood and touching earth and touching plants and just removing yourself from the everyday nonsense that is news and politics.

The repetition of mark-making, using our hands, can be soothing in its purposefulness. It quietens an anxious mind. During my interviews, I began to notice that when neighbours talked to me while holding something in their hands – a coffee cup, a dog lead, a pen – they appeared more self-confident and talkative as a result. I made a point of meeting neighbours in locations that allowed for that. We met side by side over food, walked in the park together, or I asked people to show me their creative spaces.

Making also allows for completion of a project in a way that our modern working lives, so often consumed by process and systems, doesn't always provide. There is something validating about the regularity of commitment in the social gathering of shared creative practice. When we make a date to come together on the street for knitting, dancing, singing, hula-hooping and so on, we commune in a group. We are included in the conversation.

In the middle of the street at no. 100 Constitution Street is Post Electric Recording Studio, owned by my neighbour Rod, founding member of indie rock band Idlewild. When Idlewild's debut album *Hope Is Important* achieved commercial success in 1998, Rod needed somewhere to call home when he wasn't touring with the band. He bought his first flat within the converted Assembly Rooms on Constitution Street after falling in love with *the sweeping Hollywood staircase* inside the common hallway. Much of his later solo material was written and recorded within the flat.

Rod still feels creatively at home on the street. We chatted inside the Post Electric Studio where, away from the digital mixing board of levels and faders, the studio has a homely quality with rugs, house plants and postcards of his music idols stuck on the fridge door.

Constitution Street seems to be alive with arts and music and musicians, and certainly the bars and restaurants where a lot of them, me included, hang out. No matter how many times I've moved away, [the street] seems to draw me back, weirdly.

He told me that, once a shy adolescent who felt terrified when first performing on stage, he is now a passionate advocate for the power of music-making to boost mental health and has helped set up music charity The Fruit Tree Foundation to support others finding their voice.

It's quite self-indulgent. I mean, you're kind of just assuming that every-body wants to hear what you've got to say. But it is cheaper than going to a therapist.

I wanted to hear more of what Rod had to say. Idlewild had a hit single

'Love Steals Us From Loneliness', which Rod explained was partly about how connection with others helps us get the best out of ourselves.

Singing uses a different part of the brain to speech, which is why recalling old familiar songs can be such an emotional trigger for people with dementia and why singing can also help those with stammers become more confident communicators. The familiarity soothes unsettling anxiety. In realising the right to self-expression, we regain a sense of keeping pace with change in the world and we find new shades of meaning in the senses deployed – sound, sight, smell and touch.

Next to the taps at my bathroom sink is a small piece of Cairngorm granite. I like to hold it in my left hand while I brush my teeth with my right and feel the reassuring solidity of the cold, square-faced sides of rock. If I screw my eyes up tightly, I can see flecks of purple, blue and pink reflecting out of the steely surface and onto the bathroom mirror. The shards of condensed carbon have been split, shattered and chiselled anew by the melting of glaciers and the shifting of earth and water for millennia. The stone was here before me and it will be here long after me. Touching, holding, holding on, connects me to something bigger than myself in the anxious hours of dawn and dusk when I open and close the day at the bathroom sink. I know that a sensory connection to the raw elements of the land is important for others too.

Next to my flat on Constitution Street, the Scottish Mineral and Lapidary Club has its workshop within an old yard on Maritime Lane, one of the tributaries to the main flow of the street. The yard has always been filled with craft workshops and warehouses. It can be seen from the 1560 Siege of Leith Map and is thought to have been used as storage space for flour and margarine in the nineteenth century and by herbalists and joiners in the twentieth. Now, on weekday evenings and weekends, enthusiasts can be found hunched over microscopes in boiler suits, polishing precious stones including lumps of Grampian quartz found on club field trips.

Lapidary is the creative practice of cutting and polishing stones, silver-smithing and the faceting of gemstones. Lapis Blue is a particular blue stone found only in the Hindu Kush mountains of Afghanistan. Extremely valuable, lapis was the official divine shade of blue used to represent the Virgin Mary in Europe's medieval churches. The funerary mask worn by Tutankhamun also contains Lapis Lazuli around the eyes in imitation of the kohl makeup worn by the Egyptian pharaoh.

Inside the Scottish Mineral and Lapidary Club, there is a Saw Room, Grinding Room, Lap Room, Silver Room, Mineral Room and a display area. The orientation reads like the billing of a strip club belonging in Edinburgh's sleazy West Port. Rather, the gleaming glass cabinets and heaving bookshelves of the workshop are filled with curiosities that include fossilised shark droppings, crystals that resemble feathery fern leaves and the exotic pink and purple hues of agates. One of the world's best collections of precious stones is here on Constitution Street.

Scotland is considered the birthplace of the study of geology due to James Hutton's *Theory of the Earth*, published just before the road layout of Constitution Street as we know it today, said to have been inspired by the view of Salisbury Crags from Hutton's own street.[3] A leading figure in the Scottish Enlightenment, Hutton contributed to our understanding of the age of the earth and deep time.

Deep inside the Mineral and Lapidary Club, different mineral deposits give the stones their particular colourings and layers. The most striped of the sliced diamonds-in-the-rough remind me of satellite images taken of the planetary rings of Saturn. I have a favourite Tiger Stone ring, with marbled amber and mahogany tones, which was made in the club by a friend of my grandmother's in the 1970s. I like that the ring has now returned.

Peter, a gold-panner in a blue boiler suit, returned to the club on Constitution Street to find out how to make his daughter's wedding ring from small files of gold that he found among the silty river beds and Lewisian gneiss of Sutherland. He explained that *it's not the value of the stone, it's the value you put into the stone.*

Next to Peter, I met June, dressed in a red boiler suit and concentrating on a faceting machine, much like a potter at the wheel. She let me feel the texture of the different gradients of diamond discs she uses to sharpen and smooth stone edges. Many of the club's stones are sourced from specialist dealers around the world but the cabinet drawers also contain ancient volcanic deposits from when Edinburgh's hills were once spewing out molten lava thousands of years ago. Here, in small fragments within a dark workshop, there is glitter and gold dust from silt and sand gilding the edges of Constitution Street.

Before the second dry dock was built at the foot of the street in 1774, considerable silt and sand was exposed with the high tide. A racecourse stretched along the shoreline from Constitution Street to Seafield where the sewage treatment facility is now located. Celebrated in the poem 'Leith Races'[4] by Scots Enlightenment poet Robert Fergusson, the races came to be known for drunkenness, fighting and vandalism and were eventually moved further along the coast to Musselburgh.

Today's debaucherous behaviour on the street was satirised in a site-specific adaptation of Chekhov's *The Seagull* as part of the 2017 Edinburgh Fringe Festival. Performed within the empty St James Church at no. 119 Constitution Street, the production involved a cast of lost souls climbing walls with harnesses and scaffolding, head-banging to a punk soundtrack and thrashing about in a specially installed Russian lake that flooded the back of the church.[5] The play retold a classic story in an unpredictable, messy way.

Watching the increasingly chaotic drama unfold on the stage reminded me of contemporary politics at home and abroad, where unpredictability has been a defining feature. In 2014, the arts and cultural sector in Scotland was widely regarded as being predominantly, although not exclusively, in favour of Scottish independence. Artists generally favoured constitutional change over the status quo.

Rod from Post Electric Studio was unusual in being an artist who spoke out publicly as a likely No-voter ahead of the Scottish independence referendum. As someone who switched from No to Yes, I sympathised with Rod's feelings. Rod said he felt caught between split loyalties for his English and Welsh upbringing and a left-leaning thirst for doing politics differently. He described himself as a *generous No*. Emotionally, in his heart, he felt British but he was eventually persuaded to switch to Yes when a friend explained to him that the size of the Scottish electorate, compared to that in England and Wales, would never materially impact upon the choice of government at Westminster.

> *I wanted independence but I felt bad for leaving. Maybe like two weeks before the vote, I changed to Yes.*

At the time of the independence referendum in September 2014, Rod was producing an album in New York. He went to watch the results on TV in the Iona Bar in Brooklyn while on the phone to fellow band member Roddy Woomble who lives on the isle of Iona in Scotland.

> *It was weird how in that space of time I had switched my vote and how disappointed I was. I'd sort of realised how much of that was always the way I was going to have voted and I was maybe just clinging onto this emotional attachment to the UK.*

Many other English-born voters, including neighbours and journalists Vicky and Chitra, talked about how the layering of different national identities – Anglo/Scottish/Indian in their respective mixes – made their eventual Yes votes far from straightforward. The emotional deliberations were complicated further by both women wanting to explain to their Scottish-born children why voting Yes wouldn't entail separation from grandparents and cousins in England. Such are the complexities and ambiguities hidden behind the numerical results.

Chitra described the No result in September 2014 as coming as a relief to her despite having been a *soft Yes voter*:

> *The Indian in me really wanted the Union to remain intact. I just couldn't bear the thought of the countries being separated. But the Scotland-residing person in me, who is very left-leaning and progressive, was deeply perplexed and worried by the shift to the right going on down south. I wanted nothing to do with that and wanted to vote for change. So I was a very soft Yes voter.*

Many neighbours told me about having changed their minds before and after the referendum. Within the right to expression is contained the freedom and strength to make and remake our own stories and to change our minds over and over again. As we look ahead to the constitutional future, new songs will be sung and stories told, the best of which have yet to be written. In subliminal ways, the constructed space of the street will seep into all of our mark-making.

Freedom of expression will always be the making of us. It needs to be a human right enshrined in the new constitution as well as the means by which we debate its drafting. The resulting Bill of Rights will be inspired by our mark-making and, if it's to say anything by, with and for, people on the street – as it surely must do – it will take many different forms in poetic verse, song and storytelling. As Peter the gold-panner told me, *It's the value you put in* that makes an object beautiful. The value of our many different voices, shown through our creative expression, will be what gives the constitution its sparkle.

No one shall be subjected to arbitrary interference with his privacy, family, home or correspondence, nor to attacks upon his honour and reputation. Everyone has the right to the protection of the law against such interference or attacks...

Article 12, The Universal Declaration of Human Rights

I don't think it matters that you're not actually blood-related. It's what part in their lives that you play.

Morven, Artist, 41 Constitution Street

The Right to Private and Family Life

Hand-Me-Downs

Burns wrote his address *The Rights of Woman* two years after the formal layout of Constitution Street. In it he wrote that *Europe's eye is fix'd on mighty things, the fate of Empires and the fall of Kings; while quacks of State must each produce his plan, the Rights of Woman merit some attention.*[1] A notorious philanderer and absent father, he is a controversial cheerleader for the women's rights movement. Suggesting that women need men's protection and, later in the same poem, that women have a right to be admired, is patronising at best, but the poem was strong stuff for the Masonic halls and supper clubs of Edinburgh at the time. Over 250 years later, the rights of women still merit more attention amidst the mighty fuss and fate of Empires. In January 2017, we women took to the streets to make ourselves heard, in our own words.

It is a political act to be in the world as our full selves. It involves taking risks and protesting. The word protest is rooted in the positive act of giving testimony, of bearing witness to moments of change. Reflecting on the march exactly one year on, I realised that sometimes acts of protest are deliberate, individual acts in isolation and sometimes they are part of a collective momentum. Resistance to inequality anywhere is always intersectional because we do not exist separately from one another. Side by side on the street, our different layers of identity are interwoven like threads of yarn knitted, handed down and reshaped into many hats for our many versions of self.

The Women's March at the start of 2017 was a worldwide protest for women's rights including reproductive rights and gender equality. In America, it was the largest single-day protest in the country's history, planned to coincide with the inauguration of a President who boasted about grabbing women by the genitals and who campaigned to roll back reproductive rights and restrict a woman's right to choose. This mattered at home as well as across the Atlantic. Prime Minister Theresa May was the first foreign leader to meet with the new President. She held his hand.

Walking hand in hand from Constitution Street to the Edinburgh Women's March were neighbours Chitra, Claire and myself. I remember that Chitra was wearing new, red trainers and that she seemed to be bouncing along the pavement like a little girl with a secret she was desperate to share. It didn't take long before her partner Claire relented and said, *Go on, tell her the news…* I learnt that I was an honorary member of my neighbours' growing family on the occasion of the Women's March.

We three nasty women reached the American Consulate on Regent Terrace in time to admire the slogans painted on homemade banners held aloft by thousands of other women, men and children. *We Shall Overcomb. Yer Ma Was An Immigrant Ye Bawbag. Get Your Small Hands Out of my Womb. A Woman's Place is in the Resistance.*

Beyond the placards, the grand sweep of Georgian townhouses with their consulates and merchant offices faced directly onto the Radical Road of Edinburgh's Holyrood Park. This built heritage of institutionalised patriarchy sits opposite an ancient, volcanic monument that is older than gender itself. Our city's Radical Road seems to cut into the living mountain like stretch marks on a body that has experienced love, pride and pain. This desire-line encircling Arthur's Seat is made from centuries of human walking on the city hill – our daily constitutionals.

It was a bright winter's day in postmodern Scotland at the start of a new year. The crag of red sandstone cliffs to the left of us looked gnarled and knobbly, as though part of a long finger attached to the clenched fist of the hill's summit – one finger pointing towards the North Sea and three curling back into the city centre, accusingly.

Scotland has come a long way in terms of gender equality and recognising that private and family life comes in many forms. It is said to have one of the most LGBT-friendly parliaments in the world. Three gay men and women were the leaders of the three main political parties at the time of the march. The leader of the Scottish Conservatives, Ruth Davidson, later announced that she and her wife were expecting a baby together. However, all these political leaders have spoken publicly about receiving regular homophobic abuse on social media and elsewhere. The same is true for politicians from ethnic minority backgrounds who regularly receive racist abuse. There are still no MSPs who are women of colour in Holyrood. Our representative democracy therefore falls short in knowledge and life experience.

In my street conversations, I discussed intersectionality, including racial identity and sexual identity, with neighbour Chitra.

> *In the church garden, there's an older, white Scottish man who drinks in there pretty much every day. He's very unthreatening. But, yeah, he gave me the whole, 'Where are you from?' and said some dodgy things about the Ganges. I'm not letting him have that space. I've got as much right to be there as him... There's a sort of weird pact of silence that goes on because there's so much shame attached to racism, and the kind of people that you would tell about it tend to be, you know, the people you're close to and are horrified by it, so you just think, why upset people?*

She was right, of course, to claim her space in the garden and in perceiving that I would be upset to know she had experienced racism. While laws against hate speech can be enforced now in a way that they couldn't when the first human rights treaties were agreed, there is still a big account-ability gap in ending racism, as experienced every day on the street.[2]

Domestic and international case law has reflected some of the broader, societal shifts regarding prejudice and discrimination. For example, the expansive interpretation of the right to private and family life strikes at the heart of our relationship with the state. It concerns how the state respects, protects and fulfils our identity in law and our right to be free from discrimination. Also contained within the right to private and family life is the right to love the people we choose to. Women with other women, men with other men, and those who don't identify with binary gender classifications, now hold hands walking along Constitution Street where before they might not have felt safe doing so.

Further, the law provides that public bodies including schools, health boards, prisons and courts must not act in contravention of the right to private and family life and other European Convention rights brought into force by the UK's Human Rights Act.[3] The Human Rights Act is also special in protecting not only UK citizens but all those who stand on UK soil, at home or in foreign territory held under UK control. It is the very essence of rights *in situ*.

Plans to repeal The Human Rights Act in favour of a diluted British Bill of Rights were put on hold when the Conservatives lost their Parliamentary majority in the snap General Election of June 2017.[4] Safeguards protect-ing human rights therefore remain in place for now but the act is under continuous attack by the right-wing press. The recurrent media narrative is one that portrays human rights as belonging to the apparent undeserving or scrounging, further stoking a dangerous 'them and us' dichotomy.

In the ebb and flow of our private and public selves, what we chose to reveal and what we prefer to keep hidden goes to the heart of autonomy and protest. Choices as simple as whose hands we reach for in moments of change can become a defiant act of protest.

Close to home on the Women's March in 2017, I held hands with my neighbours so not to become separated in the mass of protestors. Bereft of a placard, an older woman and veteran of the feminist movement, whom I had never met before, held out her hand and offered me a pink knitted hat, its top corners folded over to resemble the ears of a pussy cat. Here was a handcrafted gift and satirical nod to resistance against misogyny, passed on from one woman to another and very much resembling something a grandmother would knit for a newborn. It felt good to receive and, I imagine, good to give. I put on the woollen hat and smiled at the slight swell of my friend's belly beside me. We took a souvenir photograph of three, soon to be four, friends. Friends, after all, are part of the family life we choose to keep close.

Friends, neighbours and strangers linked hands and arms in the throng of the crowd. Excited children sat atop tree branches and fence posts to take in the full size of the protest, knowing that they were witnessing something special, perhaps to tell their own daughters and sons about one day. We strained to hear speeches from activists shouting into megaphones outside the American Consulate. Chitra, Claire and I were connected to women at other marches taking place on streets and cities across the world. Chitra explained why the protest was so important to her:

I just had to do something. Suddenly we are living in this time again when it really matters that you stand up. It's not just about 'clicktivism' and signing petitions online – there's something really powerful about actually going out and standing shoulder to shoulder with other people. And I loved that it [the march] was organised and led by women as well – it just

seemed so powerful — because it's always, in any kind of right-wing model
or dictatorship, it's always women's rights that are threatened first, along
with LGBT rights.

The year that began with the Women's March ended with the #MeToo
and #TimesUp campaigns in which millions of women around the
world shared personal experiences of sexual abuse following public
accusations against major Hollywood figures and politicians. After
decades of feeling silenced by shame or a mistaken politeness — of not
making a fuss — it felt like something was finally turning in the redress
of systemic imbalances of power. For me, my personal stand had a lot to
do with the increased confidence that comes with growing older and
being less willing to passively put up with abusive behaviour. I asked
other women from the street if they shared my optimism about change.
Neighbour Robyn agreed that 2017 was a momentous year for women's
empowerment but saw it as part of longer-term, gradual change.

I suppose I don't necessarily see it as a line like that because I feel — being
a little bit older than you — that I have a kind of sense of things changing
slowly. Yes there are times when things take a big jump and then things sort
of change quite a lot or they become exposed which pushes things to change.

We want our complex selves to be seen, heard and counted in the world.
In exposing abuses of power by men in the film industry, politics and
big business, the women and men that spoke out and stood up in 2017,
empowered others not to take their human rights for granted. The feminist movement was strengthened and emboldened. But the events and
campaigns also highlighted an evident crisis for masculinity and what it
meant to be a man with all the vulnerabilities and sensitivities that belong

to men as well as women.

Scotland has had a pervasive culture of abrasive masculinity, where for too long men have dominated public life while often being absent from family life. This is beginning to shift, as traditional notions of masculinity soften and society and politics become increasingly feminised.

Sandy from Constitution Street is a sixty-two year old, white, Scottish man. He drinks in the Port O' Leith bar. He was a trade union shop steward and has been a member of both the Communist Party and then the SNP. He is also a heterosexual man who sometimes likes to dress in women's clothing. In his blog called *Silver Fox in a Frock* he writes frankly and bravely about his personal journey to be accepted for the man that he is. For Sandy, this has been a process and not a single event, in which he has sought to integrate his private and public identities.

> *What does it mean to be a man if it's not the sort of macho-aggressive kind of an approach? Is it purely softening that behaviour and taking your turn with domestic chores? It's got to be something more than that. I just hope that my path will provide others with a glimpse of another way of achieving peace and an integration of who they truly are.*

Private and family life is fluid and complex. It rarely fits neat binary segmentation. Indeed, the first sentence of the Preamble to The Universal Declaration of Human Rights states simply that 'we are all members of the human family'. Sometimes Sandy choses to dress in clothes traditionally seen as being masculine and at other times he prefers wearing those regarded as women's dress.

The old Port O' Leith bar on Constitution Street was the drinking den for the archetypal brutalised, hard-man in industrial Scotland. I used to find it an unforgiving place to walk into alone. For anyone experimenting with the way gender norms are expressed in clothing, it would have been very risky terrain. So it was an act of considerable personal testimony that for the closing night party at the Port O' Leith, Sandy wore a favourite kilt with bright red lipstick and high heels. He walked into the bar arm in arm with former landlady Mary and received a warm, neighbourly welcome.

> *I've felt anxiety in my life but much, much less these days. That's because I feel I've been through this route of integration. My anxiety was straddling that divide, that split.*

Sandy and I agreed that while we felt a nostalgic tenderness regarding the end of an era at the bar, an unexpected and welcome change which has come with the modernisation of the building has been the revealing of street-level windows. Where once there were metal bars across the window frames and frosted glass that concealed the inside from the outside, now we can see one another. Stepping in or out, transitioning from private to public space, feels much safer. I thought that this was solely an observation of my fellow women from the street but Sandy said the bar now feels a much less threatening place for men too. He met his partner in the newly reopened Port O' Leith. *And she used to be a No voter!*

There is one person who knows more about the street and the different political leanings of its residents than anyone else. Postman Craig has delivered our mail for over twelve years. The street is a popular beat for postal workers because of the mix of residential and commercial properties and being *not too posh,* which keeps the volume of online shopping packages lower than elsewhere. The tradition of posties choosing their preferred street in an auction, according to seniority and length of service, remains from the days of strong unionisation in the Royal Mail. Craig explained to me that *being seen and not seen* on the street gives him a unique insight into change.

When telling neighbours about my constitutional project, I left hand-written notes of introduction in letterboxes and stairwells. Eventually, and in different ways, I got personal replies to all of my letters. This made me hopeful that people are reviving the sensible habit of handwritten post.

Recognising the slant of an inky scrawl on an envelope, noting the franking mark that connects one street to another and then receiving the sentiment inside of being held dear will never be replaced by instant, digital messaging. Letter-writing has long been a campaign tool favoured by human rights activists too. It sends a message of hope to those wrongly detained or exiled and it signals to human rights abusers that someone is watching.

The habit of letter-writing is also a part of my self-care practice. Every year on my birthday, I write and send myself a letter to be opened the following birthday. Over the years, these birthday letters have become a way of punctuating the passage of time with self-reflection. The anxieties that preoccupy my mind one year are rarely as significant twelve months on.

Of course, I didn't need to explain any of this to postie Craig. He already knew. Craig had previously confessed to me that he always reads my post-cards — occasionally remarking on a particularly bold choice of image sent to me by my grandmother — but I didn't realise the scale of the voyeurism that goes on in the Royal Mail sorting office every morning.

Everyone reads the postcards. Obviously! It starts at the primary sorting office. We all gather round to look at the interesting ones. Women always write very dense postcards. Men's postcards are like 'yeah, yeah, two lines' whereas women write whole novels squished into postcards. It makes you think it must have taken them ages to write that small for that long. Guys are crap. Girls mostly write postcards.

It was guys and girls who returned my street postcards. I soon amassed a large box of replies. Some became regular correspondents and one, the owner of a café at number 42 Constitution Street, became my partner.

Our love letters, bills, court citations and postal ballots all pass through Craig's hands. He also has main door keys to all of the tenement blocks. The good news for protecting our right to privacy of home and correspondence is that we can trust him. He has signed The Official Secrets Act. In the event of a nuclear attack, the Post Office at no. 6B Constitution Street would become the administrative control centre for the area. It is therefore always a good idea to be friendly to the postal workers. Craig credits his positive attitude to the absence of any hassle he has encountered on the doorstep.

If you go into a place with a crap attitude, you're going to get crap right back at you. If you've got a generally upbeat attitude to things, if you're smiling and happy, people don't tend to want to get in your face with stuff. But if you're already miserable and crappy, then folk are going to sense that there's nothing to stop them from getting in your face with stuff.

Craig's no-nonsense attitude has served him well. The capricious pace of constitutional change in recent years has made for an increased workload for postal service workers. Craig and his colleagues have hand-delivered the campaign materials and ballot papers in increasingly heavy mailbags. An undecided voter in the Scottish independence referendum in 2014 until he got to the ballot box, Craig told me that he didn't mind the extra baggage in his mailbag. With more doorstepping than a politician, his polling predictions were mixed. The Edinburgh North and Leith electoral ward voted No to Scottish independence (60%) and Remain (78%) to the European Union referendum.[5]

> *I think it was worth it. It was a great time for Scotland. I was a Yes voter eventually but I wasn't a right-on Yes voter. I could get where No folk were coming from. I knew mostly how people would vote. Some surprises, to be fair, but mostly I could tell.*

The official Leith coat of arms on any souvenir postcards Craig might deliver features a mother holding a newborn child, which may be the Virgin Mary and baby Jesus. They are seated in a boat together sailing in a choppy sea. Perhaps like in the original biblical story, sometimes we chose family and sometimes it chooses us by surprise.

The street itself is a sort of extended family. Not in a homespun, idolised way but in a tough coexisting of our dysfunctionality. Living or working side by side, we are constantly compromising and tolerating one another's personal and public space. We get continually lost and found together. This can prompt familial types of jealousies, rivalries and allegiances but more than anything, when our neighbours accept us for who we are and with all the baggage that we carry around, there is love. Different types of love – romantic, friendship and familial.

Like me, my neighbour Robyn doesn't have children of her own but is intimately involved in the care and upbringing of children nearby. Robyn is a trained doula, supporting mothers and families in the delivery of babies and postnatal care. She estimates that she has been involved in the delivery and care of between thirty and forty babies, including the home-birth on Constitution Street of our neighbour Vicky's second son, now eight.

I love it. I totally love it. I mean it's the best, having someone on your street. It doesn't get better than that if you know you're going to get a call in the middle of the night and can walk down the road.

Robyn interlaced her fingers to make the shape of a net or cradle when describing to me what being a doula involves.

I'm like this pair of hands that sort of holds people. Kind of a cradle...I suppose yeah, I'm cradling people...energetically or emotionally, even if it's not physically. Often it can be physical – there's lots of cradling when babies are born – but sometimes I'm doing that for the woman as well.

Robyn hosts a monthly Moon Circle with other women to ritually mark the arrival of a new moon. She invited me to join neighbours at a Moon Circle held within her house on the street. The evening began with us sitting in a circle introducing ourselves, one by one, as being a daughter and a granddaughter – giving the full names of our parents and grand-parents – and then as a mother, sister and so on as applicable. Sitting in a circle, our personal anxieties were voiced, intentions set and candles lit to hold a light for people missed or in our thoughts. It felt spiritual and like a sort of initiation into a street sisterhood.

Also at the Moon Circle, was my neighbour Vicky. Back in her home, she pointed to the corner of the family sitting room where her son was born in a planned home-birth with postnatal support from Robyn as doula. She told me that it wasn't until her own children started school in Leith that she started to feel at home in the area.

I feel more like I belong than I have in a long time, despite the busyness. And yet there's all this stuff going on in the world.

Constitution Street is a busy street. We live within its busyness and become a part of it. Vicky emphasised that there is no mute button or filter that she can turn on to protect her children from the hectic road.

> *My kids have seen and heard things that I would not have, cause I lived in the countryside at a young age. They've seen a lot of drunks, they've seen a lot of drug users. But you know at the same time, and I might be wrong, I actually feel really safe here.*

During my own busyness on the street, I had become obsessed about the safety of another family group – a family of swans in the space where the Water of Leith river meets the sea. In the springtime, seven white, fluffy cygnet chicks had emerged from the cocoon of the river bank. Swans mate for life and the committed parents kept the cygnets protected within huge wing feathers. The established family looked ready to take on the world. Yet as the year rolled on and the family took its chances along the slipstream of discarded plastic, shopping trolleys, glass bottles and the natural elements, seven became six then eventually four. Watching from the quayside, the survival of these four, newly adolescent swans seemed intrinsically linked to our own perseverance in the harshest of Scottish winters. For all of us, persevering through another year in Leith depended on an extended family network of support.

We are connected by our humanity in the disheartening, disorientating swim of the time in which we live. Humankind. Human and kind. Both words concern family. We have something in kind when it is familiar and relational. Human beings inherently want to get along with one another, to lean into the good and kind. It simply feels better than being unkind.

My neighbour Morven, the artist, has taught me a lot about kindness. She passes under my window each morning in her red velvet cloak while walking her youngest child to school, her long plait of silver hair swaying in time to her stride. I call her Little Red Riding Hood.

Morven is a mother of five children and grandmother to three. Inside her flat, every inch of the fridge door is covered with family snaps. I asked her to tell me about the faces smiling back at us as I leant into the fridge in search of milk for our tea during an interview. Morven proudly told me all about her three biological children and two adopted children, who she took into her family when the girls' mother, a former neighbour on another street, died suddenly at a young age.

> *They all call me Morv, even my own lot. My older two started doing it because it was easier for the others. I didn't want them to call me Mum right at the start because they needed to speak about their real mum. I just had them all call me Morv, which is a bit kind of naff bohemian! Anyway, that's what they do.*

Like many of us, Morven didn't know the area before moving here. In our conversations, she talked engagingly about difficult things that had happened to her family before the move but she edited the autobiographical narrative into the genre of funny anecdotes rather than memoir. I had the impression that she was trying to care for me, as much as to protect herself, in the delivery of her storytelling.

> *Things keep going. The world keeps turning, doesn't it? No matter what dreadful things are happening, you come out the other side of it. Is there such a thing as a normal family?*

On New Year's Day each year, Morven paints the surfaces of pebbles from the beach with her youngest daughter and leaves them on doorsteps along the street. *So somebody else can find them. You know, little acts of random kindness.*

I don't think there is ever anything random about acts of kindness. These are the actions of a highly mindful, sensitive person, for whom knowing and loving neighbours is part of her family values. I wrote Morv a thank you card and she stuck it on her fridge door next to the family snaps.

A snapshot of today's street-life with our civil partnerships, same-sex parenting, single-parenting, adoptive-parenting and non-binary gender would be unrecognisable to previous generations when the international human rights framework was first developed. The street-family portrait highlighted to me the different ways in which we are choosing to live our private and family lives – each as valid as the other. I saw progressive, baby-steps toward a more equal and inclusive society.

At the end of 2017, The National Records of Scotland published the most popular baby names registered that year, as well as some more unusual choices. Alongside Leia and Thor, names that presumably inspired by the big screen, there were Scottish baby names with a uniquely consti-tutional slant, such as Bella Caledonia and Bonnie-darling. At home on Constitution Street, Chitra and Claire welcomed the arrival of baby Clova. The little girl was named after a peaceful Angus glen – a good place for walking and the wearing of knitted, hand-me-down hats. Love always trumps hate, in life and law.

Everyone charged with a penal offence has the right to be presumed innocent until proved guilty according to law...

Article 11, The Universal Declaration of Human Rights

Human rights, it's across all spectrums isn't it?
It protects me as well as Joe Public.

Mark, Police Officer, 81 Constitution Street

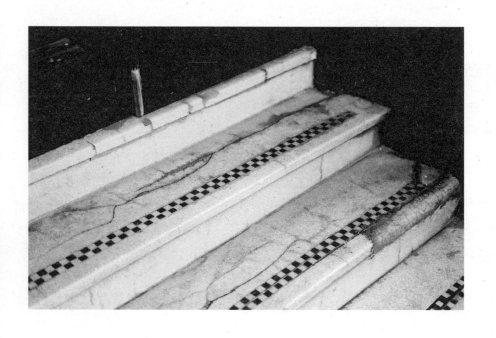

The Right to Justice

Street Haunting

In Virginia Woolf's 1927 essay 'Street Haunting: An Adventure in London', the narrator imagines the secret lives of others as she walks through the wintry, lamp-lit streets of Bloomsbury.

'What greater delight and wonder can there be than to leave the straight lines of personality,' she asks, to feel 'that one is not tethered to a single mind, but can put on briefly for a few minutes the bodies and minds of others.'[1]

As flaneuse on Constitution Street, I set out on an adventure in Leith to discover if my lamp-lit street was haunted. I already had an inkling that this might be the case but the cells of the Leith Police Station at no. 81 seemed a good place to gather evidence. Former Community Police Officer PC Mark Muir gave me the tour.

Mark has been in the police service for twenty-three years, most of which time he has spent on the beat in Leith. It is clear that Mark feels a tenderness towards the street and loves sharing his knowledge of the former Town Hall building.

The pub opposite the station used to be a notorious dive called Slammers and, before that, The Copper Bowl. Crime and punishment have always clinked glasses side by side on the street. Mark confessed to regularly coming off a night shift at 7am and heading across the road to the pub. He explained that when he takes down statements and asks people where in Edinburgh they reside, the older generation of witnesses and suspects will still respond, *No, son. I was born in Leith.* Even in matters of criminal justice, there can be civic pride.

Throughout my year and a half of paying close attention to the bodies and minds of others on the street, I did a daily scan of how the street was mentioned in the press and media. Alarming headlines arrived into my email inbox each morning: *Police release CCTV footage following attempted robbery / A blaze breaks out in Leith flats / Gang raid jewellery and cash worth £100,000 from a Constitution Street flat.* The reports of crime and disorder appear alongside more mundane posts on social media about transport congestion and dog fouling.

I started to compare the different versions and noticed that they rarely corroborated. While theft, organised drug supply and housebreaking did all take place during the eighteen months on the street, my day-to-day experience was peaceful and safe. I was aware of my own subjectivity and inherent bias based on privilege and the self-selectivity of news. Previously, I had only been inside the street's police station to collect lost property. I did not want to follow Virginia Woolf's route of seeing myself as a detached observer of others.

However, I also knew from journalistic experience that if we don't tell our own stories, others, especially the tabloid press, will do it for us. With this in mind, I tried to weigh up what was fact and what was mere speculation from both the interviews and historical accounts of life on Constitution Street. I wrote it all down in my diary.

I have kept a diary all my life. My distant ancestor, Captain Smith, the cabin boy born in 1801, was also a keen diarist. A typed copy of his modestly titled *The Book of Occurrences in the Life of Captain James Smith of Edinburgh* had long sat on a bookshelf at home after my grandmother archived it while undertaking family tree research. Smith was her great,

great uncle. It wasn't until my immersion in the Leith street-adventure, that I examined the book's contents more carefully and realised that Captain Smith and I had more than journaling in common.

Born at the turn of the nineteenth century, the young James set sail from Leith as a cabin boy aged about eight. After lengthy and dangerous voyages at sea to the new worlds of Australia, Canada and West Africa, which are all chronicled in detail in his maritime memoir, he returned to Edinburgh a wealthy man. While docked in the port of Leith in August 1822, aged twenty-one, he overlapped with the arrival of King George IV to Scotland. This was the first time that a British monarch had visited Scotland in nearly 200 years. The Battle of Culloden in 1746 and the defeat of the Jacobite Rebellion was still in living memory.

Everything the King reportedly knew about Scottish contemporary culture, he had gleaned from reading Walter Scott's novel *Waverley*. Ever the self-publicist, Scott offered his services in project-managing the royal visit. He effectively turned Leith and Edinburgh into the grandest, most flamboyant of stage-sets for a romantic work of fiction, positioning Scotland as the central character in a grand spectacle of British unionism. Constitutional passions were inflamed.

It was said that a seventh of the entire population of Scotland turned out to greet the King. This may also be a statement of Walter Scott propaganda. Regardless, my ancestor Captain Smith was amongst the throng and, even better for the purposes of my own stage-set, he was walking up and down Constitution Street at the time and told me all about it in his diary.

Whoa to him that had not a white vest on or who had a dirty face – he was looked on as not being loyal. Where it was thought the Sovereign might cast his eyes on any houses or buildings that looked unseemly, it was a case of 'Down with it and clear away the rubbish'. Many a house that had stood the test of centuries and sheltered hundreds of gude folk now fell in the ever-memorable year of 1822. Scaffolds were reared in hundreds, covered with tartan, decorated with Scotch thistles wherever it was thought a peep would be got of His Majesty... A triumphal arch was raised in Constitution Street with the motto 'Hail Scotia's King'...[2]

Smith's first-hand account further described the mood on the street:

Everyone was going about with anxious looks: 'When is he comin' noo?' Leith Docks was a favourite place, visitors looking over the ships and expectantly out to sea. I daresay sleep was a stranger that night.

Celebrity culture, mass hysteria induced by a royal visit and anxious looks were as much a part of life for some in the early nineteenth century as they are now. The grand day in 1822 duly arrived and, being a somewhat dank and wet Scottish summer, the royal carriage had to be covered. Old Jacobite songs and banners were brought to requisition with the substitution of Charlie (Bonnie Prince Stuart) for Geordie. Meanwhile, Smith was *dodging about the lower drawbridge across the river – closed to prevent the crowd running from North to South Leith but by giving a shilling to the man who kept the bridge, I got an excellent standing place near the landing stage.*

With no expense spared for the grand show and social cleansing, Edinburgh and Scotland were rendered effectively broke by the royal visit. The King was in Leith for about fifteen minutes on his way to central Edinburgh, where he stayed for a fortnight before returning to London. My ancestor's memoir notes that after dispersing, the crowd clubbed together to get *a dram or a bottle of till to drink the King's health, not forgetting themselves and to have a crack at what they had seen...Fecks, Edinbrae's muckle the waur o' the King now for every ane's complainin'*. The people of Constitution Street returned to their unseemly houses and buildings, to the extent that they still stood and had been spared Walter Scott's set-design treatment.

Smith's diary matches the scene depicted in the official painting of the visit by Alexander Carse. The original painting hangs in no. 81 Constitution Street, where it covers most of a wall in the old council chamber above the police station. The large canvas is filled with human detail. It shows every corner of the Shore area densely packed with local people dressed up by Walter Scott in Rob Roy tartan. The old Leith harbour is full of ships' crews ready to welcome the monarch and on the quayside there is a small terrier dog and a pick-pocketing child. PC Muir pointed out the detail to me, remarking that *some things never change in Leith!*

And this is where *the wee story within a wee story* comes full circle. The police station is part of the old Town Hall that originated from the time just after The Leith Act 1833 re-established Leith as a separate town. Inside, there was a magistrate's court that sat on Tuesday and Wednesday and a Justice of the Peace court for lesser crimes on the other days of the week. The cells were beneath street level and were connected by a secret passageway, now bricked over, to the courts. The old chamber room was directly above and has remained largely untouched since it was abandoned on the merger of Leith with Edinburgh in 1920. The respected dignitaries of old Leith were, then as now, cheek by jowl with the prisoners; all walking the thin, straight line of personality, as Virginia Woolf put it in her street haunting.

The fake windows flush with the street pavement mask the grim reality of the cells behind them. A long, menacing pole, with a hook at one end which police officers used to scoop out dead bodies from the Water of Leith, is suspended above a cell door. And the jail was reportedly so cold that a local butcher used to use the solitary confinement cell as extra storage for his pound of flesh.

Things had gotten little better when Her Majesty's Inspectorate of Prisons paid a routine visit in the year 2000 and were, according to PC Muir, *absolutely horrified* at what they found. The cells were deemed to be in potential breach of The European Convention on Human Rights Article 3, Freedom from Inhuman and Degrading Treatment, and were immediately put out of use. Known as the slopping out cases, some of the first cases to test human rights legislation in practice in Scotland (two years before the rest of the UK through The Scotland Act 1998[3]) were brought on behalf of prisoners challenging the controversial practice of being forced to use chamber pots in their cells.[4]

PC Mark Muir recalled the first question a suspect would ask on arrest and detention being, '*What police station are we going to?*' *As soon as you said Leith, they just filled with dread.*

Mark showed me into one of the cell blocks where suspects were held. It was about 5ft by 8ft in size, with no natural light or heating. I was glad to leave the door open and then ready to step back outside again to ask the police officer more questions.

A funny story actually is that one of the last prisoners that I ever put in here had a cistern outside. You couldn't allow the prisoner to flush their own toilet, you had to do it for them and so they would buzz a buzzer. So I came up and said to the lad – because you were responsible for the prisoner – what is it? And he said, I need the toilet flushed. So I flushed it and the whole thing came down on top of me. Soaked me. He hadn't done anything to it – it's just it was so old. I got covered in…yeah, you can imagine! Gave him a laugh though!

Human rights law, including freedom from inhuman and degrading treatment, is now a part of police training. In its various sources, human rights law further protects the right to fair trial, the right to be presumed innocent until proven guilty and freedom from arbitrary arrest or detention. This is in addition to the civil right to an effective remedy for a claimant. In exploring criminal justice on Constitution Street, I have boiled all these rights down to 'a right to justice'. However, in a full written constitution, these rights would each have standalone protection.

The Leith station is one of the busiest in the UK. Mark told me about an incident where someone had thrown a tear gas canister into a crowded pub and the police took everyone inside – about forty people – back to the cells for interrogation. *It was a conveyor belt. It was horrendous.* Today, there are about eighty police officers working across shifts in the building and a diverse workforce which includes several Polish-speaking officers, reflecting the mix of people in new Leith. The major investigations team occupy all of the top floor – *they deal with murders and things* – and then the other teams that work the cars are located in the other rooms.

Searching through newspaper cuttings in the archive rooms of Edinburgh Central Library, I came across reports of a house fire and attempted murder on Constitution Street dating from 1990. I had the sick feeling before reading on that the incident would be close to home. Described by the press at the time as a *lovers' quarrel*, a woman living alone in a tenement flat in the middle of Constitution Street had petrol poured through her letter box by her ex-partner, also resident in the same tenement stair. My tenement stair. I let out an audible gasp from my reading booth in the library. The woman survived the domestic abuse thanks to her neighbours who came to her rescue on smelling smoke in the stair. Her ex-partner went to prison.

The reality of crime and our fear of it are often far-removed. When I attended the local community council meeting, I heard updates from police representatives on crimes relating to bike theft, robberies, speeding and several search warrants for cannabis cultivation and the sale of ecstasy. Leith has lost its reputation from the 1980s and '90s for heroin supply. However, while perceptions of serious crime may have changed, Mark doesn't think that the area has cleaned up its act on class A drug use altogether.

It still goes on. I mean we search houses now that I wouldn't keep a dog in. And there are still people living in those conditions. I don't think it's gone away at all. And housebreaking, shoplifting to pay for the drugs. The big Tesco gets hit all the time.

After talking to PC Muir inside the police station, I went to interview neighbours inside the Port O' Leith bar. I got chatting to Pete, a regular. Discussing crime and punishment, he told me that when too many questions get asked, *it's time to hit the mattresses.*

Lying low, hunkering down, taking stock out of view. It's what we do when we feel a bit shifty. Pete is well-liked by the bar staff because he makes and delivers homemade lentil soup as an act of neighbourly good will on cold days. When not making soup on Constitution Street, Pete has been a guest, on and off, at Her Majesty's pleasure – doing time.

We talk about doing or serving time when incarcerated. The ancient Greeks had two words for the passing of time, *chronos* and *kairos*. *Chronos* is the chronological time that we are most familiar with in the English language. It is quantitative, sequential time. Whereas, *kairos*, meaning the space between time, is qualitative. The plural of *kairos, kairoi*, means 'the times'. It is about the right, opportune moment in between two points. Factors such as our upbringing, life experiences and mental health can influence our capacity to see and understand opportune moments of change.

The chronological time is always known on my street because we have our own clock face attached to the top floor flat of the former Exchange Buildings at no. 41. The current owner, Matt, explained to me that a hatch inside the back of a bedroom cupboard leads directly to a triangle shape in the eaves where the clock is positioned. Inside a wooden box set on a plinth, there are the workings of the original clock from 1805, complete with brass plates which show that the clock was made by a local clock-maker at the same time my ancestor was passing time in Leith. Still today, the Queen pays a stipend to an Edinburgh clockmaker to keep all of the city's public clocks in working order.

It is quite magical. You go through the wardrobe, inside a box inside a box, in a little dark room. The clock has been operated from this box for over two hundred years but still looks shiny and new. I always felt quite a big sense of responsibility to make it run on time. I remember walking home one day and I saw someone look up at our clock to check the time. I got a real buzz out of that! Yes, everyone has a watch or a mobile phone these days but people still like to see the clock on the street.

The clock on the street is now powered electrically and is connected to a power socket in Matt's bedroom. He once forgot to tell a cleaner not to use the bedroom power points. When the cleaner plugged in a hoover, time on Constitution Street was stopped for the full twenty-five minutes it took to clean the room. However, people on the street beneath the clock face continued their daily passing through place and time as usual, of course.

I would often like time to stand still. Ticking clocks, sand-timers and watches are a significant anxiety trigger for me. I will often remove and hide away any wall-mounted clock in a hotel room and I only keep one digital alarm at home. The anxiety induced by ticking and ringing must be connected to feelings of control, attachment and loss. Timing, it really is everything.

In the particular moment in time in which we are living today, many of the stories told to me on Constitution Street were certainly haunting and involved injustices. Some I decided not to include here to prevent incriminating my neighbours or others. However, more often than not, I heard the stories as symptomatic of the state's failure to respect, protect and fulfil basic socio-economic rights. Stories about personal drug use and sex work were really about the right to access healthcare, not acts of criminality. Incidents of squatting in vacant properties or begging on the street were about the right to adequate housing. A failure to realise the right to work or social security was often the real story behind reports of theft.

This is how I wrote up the evidence in my diary. I have tried to do so without judgement of people themselves. Where I have judged us to be lacking, it is in our experience as a collective, constituted whole – as a nation of streets – where crime still disproportionately affects those from poorer neighbourhoods and barriers, such as the cost of legal represen-tation, can prevent fair and equal access to the law. Inherent fairness and criminal justice are not, afterall, the same thing.

And the street is officially haunted, beyond any reasonable doubt. I know this to be true because a ghost hunting tour bus is parked every night in the forecourt of the garage, located one block from the police station. The bus is painted a ghoulish black and the sides decorated with caricatures of axe-wielding skeletons. The tour company's website boasts of 'frightening tales told in the shadow of Walter Scott's Edinburgh as part of a comedy theatre horror show.'

I tried several times to meet with one of the tour guides for an interview but appointments scheduled by email fell through. I began to doubt the existence of any real people because, although not always parked in the same position, I never saw a driver or passenger aboard the bus. None of the Leith area of Edinburgh, with its many stories of crime and punishment, justice and injustices, is on the advertised tour route. Perhaps that is exactly as it should be, leaving something of the secret lives of others to the imagination.

(There is no explicit Right to the Environment in The Universal Declaration of Human Rights.)

It's just about being out there. I just like being out there.

Vicky, Journalist, Leith Community Croft

The Right to the Environment

Grassroots Change

Things had been left unsaid and done in a wintry way. And so, the rite of spring came late to Constitution Street in 2018. The few trees that line the pavement held their buds tight and their secrets close. Then finally in April, the petals were given up and drifts of frothy pink cherry blossom caught the breeze and began to land all around us once again, even in the grimiest of street gutters, as though confetti for an annual celebration. Blossom, so much a part of spring that it's a cliché.

News at the time spoke of two old men of war holding hands on the Korean border. In the television footage, I heard bird song punctuated by the sound of camera clicks. Late April and then into early May is a time of cathartic release for those who survive a cold winter and choose to stick around to dance to nature's new tempo.

The repeated checks and balances of nature, as writer and marine biologist Rachel Carson described it, is the assurance that dawn comes after night and spring, and the chirping of birds, follows winter.[1] Softly, softly, the street and its people also unfurled like ferns in a wooded, urban glade. The pretty petals that stained the pavements pink were nature's reminder of the temporal way of things – that nothing, and no one, last forever.

I wasn't celebrating. Knee-deep in the silt and soil of a scraggly patch of grass, I was flailing my limbs around like a whirling dervish in a dance of loss after my grandmother's funeral. She had died suddenly and unexpectedly. I was heartbroken. It is not unusual to lose a grandparent at my age but she wasn't a usual person and she had been a constant and central figure in my life. I had lived with her in 2008 before moving to Constitution Street. Grief is a wild, wild storm. It howls all round while we keep plodding uphill, stumbling on the scree and grasping for a safe hand that is now out of reach for an indefinite period of time. The familiar ground on which I had walked suddenly felt raked over.

Of course loss is everywhere when you start to notice it. Good people do die on beautiful spring days. My neighbour Maddie lost her own grandmother on the same day. I was walking across the road on my way to comfort Maddie when I received news of my bereavement. The generations in my family had shuffled forward and four rows had become three. I found myself tripping up on my use of the present tense instead of the past. That someone of the Northern Hemisphere, who knew all the birds and plants by name, would chose not to wait for the festival of spring cherry blossom to descend, did not make any sense.

Part of remembrance in grief is going back over the life we knew, searching for signs to explain and accept the recurring mystery of loss. Isobel and I were very alike in lots of ways but different in one crucial respect. She was not an indecisive or hesitant person. In the March of 2018, she had sent me a postcard on which she signed off her message 'P.S. I am finally parting with my favourite postcard.' On the front was an image of a sculpture at the Scottish National Gallery of Modern Art, entitled *Tourists*. My ever-vigilant postman, Craig, remarked on the card when delivering it but I failed to spot the thinly-veiled clues in the familiar handwriting landing on my doormat. Gran and I were regular correspondents over thirty years and I guessed that she had lots of favourite postcards, much as I know that she had other favourite granddaughters who were also penpals.

After the funeral, it seemed natural, essential, to get out of my own head and into somewhere else. I pulled off my black dress and heels and went to physically exhaust myself digging and sweating in the filth of a spring evening at the Leith Community Croft next to Constitution Street. A croft is an enclosed area of land used for small-scale food production, in tune with the seasons and where neighbouring growers lend one another a hand.

The symbology of earth to earth down at the croft wasn't lost on me. Mud therapy. As though getting dirt under my nails and grass stains on my jeans could cleanse the mulching potency of guilt, regret and anger that comes with a shock bereavement. I tore into thistle and nettle weeds, uprooting and shaking their thorny, stinging tentacles. The ringed, sinewy bodies of earthworms left behind in the soil became rudely exposed to the light and appeared almost translucent. I then pushed brassica saplings into the newly made gaps with the heel of my palm. Four new rows of kale and sprouts for an autumn harvest.

Streaks of dark brown clay mixed with saline streaked across the backs of my hands and cheekbones like tribal warpaint. I was doing battle with myself. All the while, my small black dog, Bonnie, was at my side. She whimpered with concern and licked my face with her warm tongue and malty breath.

Then as the air began to cool and the daylight folded its corners inward, my boyfriend arrived at the park to find me spent but somewhat purged, squatting in the middle of a newly-planted bed. I had taken back control of some of the disordering chaos of loss. Or so it felt. We watered the fragile saplings together and then walked the short distance home. I cried my last for the day standing in a steaming hot shower, watching mud swirl with soap suds in the shower tray, the momentary distraction of nurturing new life having worn off and the numbing sensation of an absence returning.

There were, of course, other lighter, days at the croft in 2017–2018. Days filled with learning about myself, my neighbours and the shifting lie of our land. Unlike other areas of the city, few of our tenement flats on Constitution Street have communal back gardens, such was the pressure on available land for housing during the overcrowding of Leith in its seafaring heyday of the nineteenth century. Old maps from the archives of the National Library of Scotland hint at narrow market gardens, much like those still found in some Middle Eastern cities, extending from the back of dwellings in the medieval Kirkgate. Traces of these gardens have long since been replaced by carparks and budget supermarkets.

Just as the planet cannot sustain limitless growth, there is simply not enough space in the city for everyone to have a private garden. The balance of private luxury versus public amenity has become skewed to the detriment of the many. Instead, we have a type of commons in the park.[2]

Each plot is tended by a collective of community growers. I belong to the 'F' group of plotters, alongside other women who live in tenements without private gardens, in or around Constitution Street. It is not a pristine wilderness and digging deep in the plot on mild evenings and weekends, we regularly unearth cans, condom wrappers, syringes and glow sticks beneath the silty soil that was formerly sand dunes along the ancient shore. The communal greenhouse was even rumoured to have been commandeered by nightime sex workers for a short while. But this land is our land. It has soft borders and is held in common.

Like me, my neighbour Vicky also perseveres with the green space we have available. We discussed our mixed successes with growing different vegetables and the trickier business of attachment.

For me it's all about the group. One year, I planted an artichoke plant and it grew quite well. I was really keen on having these artichokes, and then

we lost the plot — it went over to someone else, the artichoke, cause it needs
a few years. Then we tried to shift the artichoke and it died. I realised that
I couldn't get too attached to any individual plants. It's just about being
out there.

Being out there with others is what the growing space has gifted me too. Inherent to the human condition and our second nature is to be in a community of one form or another. Most of us are in multiple communities of interest and place, professional and social, digital and virtual and these sometimes overlap like concentric circles in a Venn diagram.

Communities can be slippery things to define. When I worked in human rights outreach, I would often hear politicians make sweeping statements about community empowerment and development but it was unclear to me which community or communities they were referring to. Where does a community begin and end? Is the decision-making of a community determined by those who shout the loudest?

A street community of neighbours is comparatively easy to define because a street has obvious start and end points on a map. It has a name and quantifiable members, or residents, who know that they have an address here with a street number and so belong by default.

Like a successful business or government, resilient communities need dispersed and authentic leadership, drawing upon different skill sets and life experiences. Our mutuality and adaptability are critical to the common good. Land for sharing food production and for flinging handfuls of dirt around in times of strife can offer up breathing space when dealing with life's up and downs, as well as putting food on the table.

Commoning, here on the croft, is about nurturing an interdependent ecosystem of people and nature. As Vicky said, it's about the group as much as being outdoors. It is the essence of thinking globally and acting locally.[3]

In small ways, down on the croft with neighbours, we are promoting and protecting our right to a healthy environment.

The Right to the Environment is conspicuously absent in the main human rights treaties drafted after the Second World War. There is no overt protection for the environment in The Universal Declaration of Human Rights. It wasn't that drafters could not conceive of legal personality extending beyond humans. Inanimate entities such as corporations, trusts and partnerships all already exercised rights. The omission was because the scale and pace of human destruction of nature had not yet become clear. Or not clear enough. The inconvenient truth of the irreversible damage inflicted on people and planet by mass industrialisation fell on deaf ears as global capitalism, with its unfettered growth and expansion, became the prevailing narrative of the mid to late twentieth century.

Some forty or so years ago, ecologists like Rachel Carson and Murray Bookchin sensed that the social and the natural must be understood in a new unity. That the time had come to integrate an ecological natural philosophy with social philosophy. This unity was essential, they argued, if we were to avoid ecological and human catastrophe.

Now with unequivocal evidence that global temperatures are rising to the irreversible detriment of the planet and that the world's poorest and most vulnerable people are being disproportionately impacted by the climate crisis, progress is slowly being made in linking the international human rights and climate justice frameworks. A failure to respect, protect and fulfil the right to a safe environment can have a cumulative effect on those already suffering from low-quality housing, poor sanitation and food insecurity. Our rights to adequate healthcare and housing are dependent on the right to a clean and safe environment. For example, damp, mouldy houses or the presence of dangerous chemicals, threatens the health of nearby residents.

Several national constitutions around the world do contain a right to a healthy environment, such as those of Costa Rica,[4] Brazil,[5] Colombia[6], and, more recently, France (following enactment of The Charter of the Environment[7]). The UK does not, of course, have a written constitution and there are no explicit, positive rights to, or for, the environment in our constitutionalism mix of conventions. However, the UK is a signatory of The International Covenant on Economic, Social and Cultural Rights (ICESCR). This human rights treaty includes the 'right of everyone to the enjoyment of the highest attainable standard of physical and mental health' and obligates member states to take reasonable steps to improve 'all aspects of environmental and industrial hygiene.'[8] This comes close to a right to the environment but, as the UK has not directly incorporated the ICESCR into domestic law, it is a hard thing to enforce.

This may change, however. In Scotland, there is momentum from some in the legal profession and civil society to expand rights promotion and protection to economic social and cultural rights, potentially within a new written constitution.[9] Scotland has an opportunity to advance human rights, including a right to the environment and the right to an effective remedy where the right is breached, in this particular moment in time.[10]

Scotland's national human rights institution, the Scottish Human Rights Commission, has responsibility for holding the state to account for its implementation of human rights. The Commission introduced me to residents of Persevere Court in Leith, a tower block two streets away from Constitution Street. With support from the local tenants' association, residents have been monitoring their direct experience of human rights in relation to standards of living and the environment. The reality of pigeon waste in stairwells, poor quality insulation in housing and a lack of safe spaces in which children can play have all been documented and measured against international indicators. In this way, rights holders themselves have been empowered to hold the state to account in its obligations regarding basic living conditions.[11]

In constitutional theory, a minimum level of subsistence is required for the full functioning of a democratic society. This principle of minimum guarantee is enshrined in the founding provisions of many written constitutions around the world, including in Germany (*existenzminimum*), Switzerland (*conditions minimales d'existence*), Belgium (*minimex*) and Colombia (*minimo vital*).[12]

There is also a shift taking place in the jurisprudence of other countries as to how a healthy environment as part of a basic standard of living can be enforced in law.[13] At The European Court of Human Rights in Strasbourg, judges have held that there can be a potential violation of a person's right to private and family life where the state has failed to regulate private industry. For example, the Strasbourg court famously found against the Spanish Government for not protecting a family from toxic gases, repetitive noise and strong smells coming from a waste processing plant built only metres from the family home.[14] Similarly, in exceptional circumstances, there may be a violation of the right to life if a person's physical integrity is put at risk by the state's environmental failings.[15]

All of this jurisprudence is very human-centric of course – a person has to establish that they are a victim of a rights breach – as is the norm for human rights law in the courts. This follows the western legal tradition of individual liberties, first developed in the constitutional age of the late eighteenth century.

In the United States in 1787, fifty-five white, wig-wearing men were shut away in a closed room in Philadelphia over four, hot summer months. The text that emerged gave nothing away of the doubts, hesitations and compromises that must inevitably have been part of the sweaty deliberation process.

This historical closed-room approach contrasts with contemporary experiments in mass participation for constitutional change. For example, in Iceland following economic collapse and national soul-searching in 2008, the crowdsourcing of a written constitution began with people sitting down to talk about the basic values they shared in common with neighbours. By and large, the Icelandic drafting was not done by constitutional law experts. The drafters selected by public ballot included a farmer, a truck driver, a pastor, a filmmaker, a student and an art museum director. And the negotiations of the 114 articles did not take place in closed rooms. They debated in public meetings, on social media and even in knitting circles. After these open conversations, a constitutional council of twenty-five people (fifteen men, ten women) were elected by their fellow Icelanders and given four cold months to draft a new constitution.

Why does this matter for my community croft and surrounds in Leith? Because the resulting Icelandic Constitutional Convention opted to give legal personality to nature itself.[16] This in turn was based on the Ecuadorian concept of Pachamama, the Andean Earth goddess. In 2008, Ecuador was the first country to recognise the Rights of Nature in its national constitution.[17] Rather than treating nature as property under the law, the constitutional articles acknowledge that nature in all its life forms has 'the right to exist, persist, maintain and regenerate its vital cycles.' The environment can be named as a legal party with standing in the justiciability of constitutional rights.

I learnt first-hand about comparative examples of environmental rights from my Icelandic neighbour, Kristin, at Lamb's House. Kristin is a volunteer with The Water of Leith Conservation Trust. She explained to me that the river basin is owned privately and that the current owner, Forth Ports, has installed sluice gates to stop there being a tidal rise and fall at the docks. The silt of the riverbed can no longer flow freely out to sea, leaving it clogged and vulnerable to pollution and meaning that seals don't bathe on the riverbank as they once did decades ago.

Kristin talked enthusiastically about organising a future community buy-out of the river basin through Community Empowerment legislation in Scotland.[18] Thus far, these new statutory powers have been mostly tested by highly mobilised, rural communities, including buy-outs on the islands of Eigg and Ulva where previously there had been absent landlords. Yet more than half of Scotland's private land is still held by fewer than 500 people.[19] Holding a river basin in stewardship and trust for the collective benefit of a large, urban area could be quite radical.

With growing momentum for land redistribution and calls for the strengthening and decentralising of local democracy across Scotland, there is every potential for a future written constitution to be sufficiently radical as to include the right to the environment. Recent land reform legislation in Scotland is rooted in international human rights commitments including the European Convention.[20] A new, explicit constitutional right to the environment will have to redress the balance between private property rights and economic, social and cultural rights.

In spring 2018, close to home, I attended a meeting of the Leith Links Community Council. I listened as our elected community councillors, including fellow gardeners from the croft, police officers and concerned residents got bogged down in the realities of local planning, noise pollution disputes and shit. Lots of shit. Late spring is *the smelly season* in Leith. We were told that on warmer days the smell of fresh sewage would once again waft across the park from the nearby waste treatment facility. Sludge levels from the sewage plant risked becoming septic and, as the chair of the meeting summed up: *It isn't fresh, it's honking.*

In the past, all of the heavy industries of old Leith were dependent upon the river. After centuries of waste mismanagement, this has taken its toll on the environmental quality of the air and water. Constitution Street is now part of an air-quality management area in an effort to reduce pollution, and while air quality is improving, it doesn't yet meet safe levels by European emission standards.[21]

Where other capital cities have boardwalks, nature reserves and yachting marinas along their coastline, my area of Edinburgh has a casino, garages, a bus depot and a waste treatment works. All are in private ownership. A large-scale repurposing of this littoral zone in between sea and land is long overdue. For now, residents make the most of semi-wild, natural spaces in and around the street, such as at the croft.

The croft land was formerly clay tennis courts that had become derelict and a dumping ground for rubbish, after neglect and a lack of public investment. It was regarded as a dangerous no-go area. It has gradually been restored by my neighbours to become a thriving, safe environment for all to enjoy throughout the seasons. It is a place for us to leave behind the busyness of the street.

We hold land like the croft in trust for the next generation. Nature has no need for borders and flags. It is far more important than any national politics. The right to the environment is the greatest issue of our time and certainly merits constitutional significance. Scotland could demonstrate real leadership by enshrining rights for nature itself.

Nature shows us the way to co-exist. A neighbourhood community, like a family, is a form of inter-connected ecosystem. Like all life forms, from the thorniest thistle, to a wriggling earthworm, we are dependent on other creatures.

I depended on good neighbours to learn from, and to listen to me, during the ups and downs, loves and losses that I experienced during 2017 and 2018. While I dug into the local history, conversation at the croft went round and round like the seasons themselves. Through it all, I needed outdoor space in which to breathe and to think. During disorientating change – personal and political – walking on common ground was my constant, my permaculture.

The brassica saplings that I had planted in my dance of grief earlier in the spring were soon munched by pigeons. I had failed to protect the young, tender leaves with netting and pegs. The hungry birds needed to eat the first shoots of green more than I did. However, the stumps of the plants survived into the summer to become a full salad crop in autumn, thanks to a fellow crofter and neighbour. He saw my inexperienced error and got down on his hands and knees to measure and attach a sheet of protective covering with canes. He then showed me how I could later adjust the bamboo canes as the plants grew stronger and taller. And like that, the cycle of renewal and new growth continued.

Also during the autumn, I helped clear out my grandparents' Edinburgh home, making it ready for a new family to move into. On a bedroom shelf, I found a bulging A4 folder marked 'Jemma'. Inside were thirty years' worth of letters, drawings and postcards I had sent to my grandmother. She had kept each one. Returning to sender, she gave me the surprise gift of knowing that I had been a loyal and worthy correspondent. It was another lesson in patience and acceptance.

I took the folder safely back to Leith with me, and now I don't know quite what to do with it. At the moment, the colourful envelopes and drawings from childhood-Jemma are stacked together, side by side, like seed packets from a mail-order catalogue waiting to be opened on a sunny day.

Everyone is entitled to a social and international order in which the rights and freedoms set forth in this Declaration can be fully realised...

Article 28, The Universal Declaration of Human Rights

We're going to have to come to terms with some kind of gentle, liberal Scottish Constitution that probably reflects who we are right now, not who we used to be. A street-wise kind of common sense.

JP, Theatre Director, 156 Constitution Street

The Right to Self-Determination

Taking to the Streets

On Constitution Street, I had set about exploring what the particular in one small place might reveal about universal truths in all places, to put the world to rights. Apart from occasional trips to the reading rooms of Edinburgh Central Library, I rarely strayed far from my EH6 postcode. However, in the post-referendums landscape of Scotland and the UK in 2017–2018, I knew I couldn't shy away from including the right to self-determination in an exploration of rights in practice. For this, I needed to go out and learn from streets elsewhere in the world.

In the summer of 2017, I travelled to the ancient home of democracy, Athens, and stood amongst the crowds of tourists atop the Acropolis looking down upon remains of the oldest known assembly of people, the Athenian Agora. Then in October of the same year, I went to Barcelona in Spain where the city's government is headed by former housing rights activist, Ada Calau.[1]

In the winter months, Kurdish friends came to stay with me at home on Constitution Street after their own unofficial referendum on Kurdish statehood in northern Iraq had been largely ignored by the international community.[2] I also met with the Secretary of the Icelandic Constitutional Convention when she visited Edinburgh.

All of these inter-cultural exchanges and conversations expanded my own thinking about how democracy could be overhauled, to more closely involve rights-holders – you, me, and our neighbours – in the decisions which directly affect our lives. It gave me a new perspective on how to normalise democratic engagement, so that it embodies its original Greek meaning, people power, and not something left to politicians and lawyers.

From Spanish housing cooperatives to occupations in Greek squares, the story of the commons was one told to me again and again by friends from other streets. The commons is a way of sharing resources – property, water, food, green spaces, cultural venues and public amenities – for collective good, distinct from market forces. The commons functions best when it includes a diversity of life experiences and a critical mass of people within the commons to create social and economic wealth for the benefit of all.

At first, learning about alternative approaches to democratic engagement felt like an existential threat to my understanding of a constitutional paradigm. How could small, place-based commons fit within the nation state and international relations as I had been taught to understand it as a law student? I veered from being excited by the prospect of a different way of doing politics, to feeling confused about how to relate new ideas to my own small place close to home. Then I returned to paying close attention to my neighbourhood and, once again, the street showed a way forward out of confusion.

The street is itself a form of commons. On my street, and likely also on the street where you live or work, we have a diversity of people with different skills and ideas with which to negotiate the sharing of resources. The critical mass for a functioning commons is roughly the size of a village or long street. Here on Constitution Street, our shared resources include the park, with its croft, and the civic spaces on pavements, stairs and tenement closes. We are linked to other streets, other commons, and have more than one story to tell in our expressions of self-determination.

Much of international law, including the UDHR, was negotiated and agreed in the middle of the twentieth century, when preserving national borders was a defining feature of post-war peace and security efforts. By its very nature, international law — the law drafted by representatives of nation states — does not encourage secession regions within a sovereign nation to break away. There is therefore no explicit right to self-determination in The Universal Declaration of Human Rights. Rather, Article 28 is a procedural right about the social contract between a nation state and its citizens. It speaks about power — the power and trust we place in our elected governments to respect, protect and fulfil the full range of human rights. It recognises the principle of mutuality whereby states hold one another to account in their human rights obligations. However, I think it is significant that the title of the UDHR was changed from 'International' to 'Universal' during the drafting deliberations, signifying a shift in focus from states to human beings.

One of the recurring stories that I heard in my local history research concerned power, trust and self-determination during an unofficial referendum. The *Lightning Plebiscite* in Leith in 1920 was so-called because of the pace at which the vote was organised. Hunched over a microfilm machine inside the library, I scrolled through excerpts from *The Leith Observer*, 3 August 1920.

I learnt that from the balcony of Leith Town Hall at no. 81 Constitution Street, Liberal Member of Parliament, Captain William Benn MP (father and grandfather of the Labour MPs Tony Benn and Hilary Benn) declared a proclamation to the waiting crowd below on the results of the plebiscite, or unofficial referendum. The question to determine was whether or not the independent burgh of Leith should reunite with the city of Edinburgh.

And the answer to the question, 'Should Leith remain an independent Burgh?' is…no surrender.

Benn's feisty language says something about the strength of feeling on the local matter of independence and remaining. Leithers voted 6:1 against the merger of Leith with Edinburgh in 1920 but were over-ruled by Edinburgh City Council who successfully lobbied Parliament to keep Leith within the Edinburgh city boundaries. The editorial of *The Leith Observer* was scathing in its analysis of how the popular vote was dismissed by authorities.

The House of Commons has stultified itself by its decision. The absorption of Leith in the maw of her neighbour is enforced interference and a triumph of might over right. Time, the healer, may assuage the grief and even sweeten the bitterness.

At the time in 1920, Leith had an independent police force, health board, theatre, dancehall, town hall, assembly rooms and water supply. Many civic buildings were located on Constitution Street and their original community purpose is now lost to history. However, the town hall chamber room, inside what is now Leith Police Station, is almost completely untouched since 1920. It is as though frozen in time since the summer's day 100 years ago when Leith rejoined Edinburgh against the will of the people, as today's political rhetoric would describe it.

The boardroom table is set exactly as it once was, with leather-bound placemats at the seventeen chairs around the table and portraits on the surrounding walls of the succession of white, male Lord Provosts who governed the burgh throughout its independent years, 1833–1920. The clock on a wall remains fixed at 11:55. It is therefore always the eleventh hour on Constitution Street for the relationship between Leith and its bigger neighbour, the city of Edinburgh.

I think it is also late in the day for healing the increasingly fragmented relationship between Scotland, the UK and the EU in today's constitutional arrangements. The first past the post system at Westminster and a UK population demographic dominated by south east england, results in a persistent democratic deficit at the ballot box. The Edinburgh Agreement 2012 between the UK and Scottish Governments was the constitutional mechanism that provided for Scots to exercise their right to self-determination in the Scottish independence referendum of 2014. The extent to which the UK Government must consent to a future Scottish independence referendum concerns the expansion and limitation of this right.

Some of the most enthusiastic cheerleaders of Scotland's right to self-determination during the independence referendum debate in 2014 were in Catalonia. In October 2017, I returned to Barcelona to visit Catalan friends and witness their unofficial referendum in the face of forceful, and sometimes violent, opposition from the Spanish Government.

Spain's written constitution from 1978 is not a living document like the one I would like to see for Scotland. It does not allow for amendments and is rigidly applied by the judiciary. This has included a refusal to amend Article 155 of the Spanish Constitution to allow for a self-determining for Catalans, Basques and Galicians on direct rule from Madrid versus independence.

I saw for myself the strength of feeling on all sides in Barcelona. The rain in Spain fell hot and hard in October 2017. It came as strokes of batons and rubber bullets in the streets. An umbrella broken in the crush of the crowd split a puddle into two. Its spokes bent upward like jabbing fingers demanding of the sky *Votarem!* At the entrance to Escola Pia de

Sant Antoni, I saw steel shutters crumpled in on themselves as though a fan snapped shut by assaulting hands. I saw the ballot papers – white slips raked, swept and counted, then later kicked along the streets and stuck to the soles of black boots. Sunday morning joggers like myself paused on the kerbside to take up arms on hips and knees. Our soft, sweating bodies making us believe that the people must surely be sovereign.

In Plaça de Catalunya, young independistas wrapped themselves in the flags of their grandparents. Their clenched fists boxed the air and the air gathered in close and fat with the smell of tobacco and wet pavement. Then at midnight on 1 October, darkness came creeping, seeping through the city on strike. At least, that is how I remember Spain in my autumn journal.[3]

It is easy to get carried away by long distance relationships but Catalonia is not Scotland and Scotland is not Catalonia. Civil war is not in our living memory. Further, the Scottish independence referendum was free from violence and agreed by the UK Government. Yet, the two places are linked by the right to self-determination. They are linked for me in personal ways too.

My grandfather's cousins, brothers from the Springburn area of north Glasgow, volunteered with the International Brigade on the side of the Republicans during the Spanish Civil War in 1936. Motivated to help by the newsreels in Glasgow cinemas showing poverty and bloodshed on Spanish streets, as well as undoubtedly being keen for an adventure, the brothers' stories about self-discovery in Europe were later hushed up back home in Scotland as they were branded as communists and blacklisted in the Clydeside labour market.

On Constitution Street, we have always been European to our core. In 1790, the street became the connective tissue for the mixing of people and ideas as part of city plans to ease the movement of cargo from continental ships at the docks. Still today, the street is home to a multitude of nation-alities and ethnicities. When I open my kitchen window, I hear Italian and Spanish being spoken by the visiting language exchange students passing by on their way to lessons inside the old St John's Church. I can step outside to buy squares of sticky baklava from my favourite Turkish cafés. And walking to a café, I might meet first-generation Polish families walking to Mass at St Mary's Star of the Sea Church.

We risk losing this economic, social and cultural diversity at our peril. Restrictions on the free movement of people, goods and services threaten to deter new arrivals and to make those who have settled in Scotland feel less welcome. It also limits our capacity to freely travel to other streets around the world and learn from their people and ideas. There will be potential new neighbours whom we will never come to know.

Scotland is not unique among the nations of the UK in being exposed to these risks. We could plug the accountability gap in rights protection through drafting of a written constitution for the UK, but the divisions in UK politics have shown that such deliberative process will not be possible. Or Scotland could enhance rights protection while still a devolved nation within the UK. However, the demographic need for immigration in Scotland is particularly stark. Scotland has the lowest birth rate in the UK and the population of people aged over seventy-five is projected to rise by almost 80%.[4] Any increase in population over the next twenty-five years will have to come from immigration. Full legislative control of issues currently reserved to Westminster, like immigration, foreign policy and finance, is needed to make the consti-tution comprehensive of all aspects of rights in practice.

Scots voted by nearly 2:1 in favour of remaining in the European Union with its free movement of people. Yet our future in the EU will be determined by a UK Government that most Scots didn't vote for and which told us that a vote against Scottish independence was the only way to be sure of staying in Europe. Somewhat like the Leith of 1920, contemporary Scotland was sold false expectations by the elected leaders of its immediate neighbour, in both 2014 and 2016. It is time to acknowledge that it is the end of the road for UK constitutionalism as we know it. It is time to speak up, self-organise and do things differently.

In doing things differently, we could learn a lot from looking north, to Iceland. When I met with Secretary of the Icelandic Constitutional Convention, Katrin Oddsdóttir, over supper at Lamb's House in Leith, she told me *You will not find two people who will agree one hundred percent on a constitution.* There has to be compromise and consensus in agreeing a collective expression of intent. The process of coming together to ask *How do we want to live alongside one another?* emboldened Icelanders to hold their government to greater account in how human rights are promoted and protected. *Iceland hasn't suddenly become a democratic utopia but we have a feeling in the cells of our bodies that we have social fabric and that is powerful.*

National politics in Scotland, and the UK, does not work like this. It is extremely centralised with our elected politicians representing large geographic areas and the first past the post electoral system resulting in a political culture of dominance rather than compromise. This can be particularly dicey when it comes to questions of such national importance as those of self-determination because our differences and perceptions of 'other' risk becoming magnified and distorted.

One of my own long-held 'others' on Constitution Street was the casino at the end of the road. Its position on Ocean Drive by the old entrance and exit signs to the far east of the street blocks out any view of the sea, much to my annoyance. I assumed that casinos were low-lit drinking dens frequented by seedy men after hours and owned by those who take pleasure in profiting from people vulnerable to addiction. In truth, I had never been inside a casino.

I was surprised, then, when Lynn, a businesswoman and art school graduate welcomed me at the casino reception. She was similarly surprised that I had asked her for an interview. I think she suspected I had a pre-set agenda regarding regulation and licensing. No one had ever asked her about her work and the casino's relationship to the surrounding local area.

Lynn is General Manager of the Leith branch of a Malaysian casino chain. It was early in the evening when we met and the poker tables and rows of slot machines were already busy. She showed me around the large games hall, bathed in natural light from the panoramic views of the Firth of Forth, and spoke with warmth about her customers. Lynn knows many by their first names, most of whom are shift-workers or restaurant owners wanting somewhere to unwind after their own businesses have closed for the night. She was even invited to the funeral of a former customer. For some, the casino is its own particular community.

However, Lynn confessed to me that she doesn't gamble herself. She knows the odds and is risk-averse. Sitting with her at the poker table made me reflect on the extent to which we have control over the decisions that affect us. As a card-carrying indecisive person, I am interested in what aspects of life we can pre-determine through rational thought and information-gathering and what is best left to chance, or the throw of a dice.

When placing power in the hands of elected officials to make decisions for me, I want to know that they are the best people to make those decisions and that they will put the interests of the community as a whole ahead of gambling with party political stakes. This has not been the reality in the last few years of constitutional crisis. Scotland and the UK have felt insular. We have been guilty of exceptionalism, thinking that we alone know best, that our islands in the North Sea don't need the learning from and exchange with other nations. In truth, we need these things now more than ever. National identity politics will become increasingly irrelevant in the face of climate crisis and food insecurity.

The right to self-determination – of the nation state, of city boundaries, and in the personal discovery of self that comes with travel and relationships – is about having the autonomy and bravery to know when to come together and when to break apart. In our collective journey of constitutional change, we are standing at a crossroads and are in need of leadership and a map. A new, written constitution founded on principles of international human rights law can be that unfolding map. The leadership will come from those close to home who have been guiding us in other, meaningful ways all along.

We are living through an important moment in our country's history.

Theresa May, Prime Minister, 10 Downing Street

I don't know about you but this Brexit thing, the minute that comes on the television, I just politely turn it off. It just seems to be ongoing just now, and I feel that you're not hearing all about the other news.

Margaret, Lollipop Lady, 161 Constitution Street

At a Crossroads

As my year and a half of weighing up evidence on Constitution Street drew to a close, I was informed by the vet that my most loyal and constant of street mates, Bon-dog, had an irregular heartbeat and was near the end of life. It felt like time itself was speeding up and I could do absolutely nothing to control it. I held my breath in anticipation of loss every time I opened my front door.

All across the country people felt more and more anxious too. Looming into view like a cliff-edge was the original Brexit date, 29 March 2019. There was confusion, indecision and delay in the House of Commons about a deal or no-deal scenario while political parties fought their internal pitch battles. There were daily resignations, plots and coups. Nothing was certain. Should we be stockpiling medicines and food in the event of a no-deal exit from the EU? Would it be safe to book flights to Europe? Would grants funded by the EU come to an immediate end? And more importantly, would friends and neighbours from other EU countries be made welcome? Decisiveness at this critical juncture was missing.

While the news rolled on, I was at home, nursing Bonnie and matching up my diary accounts from the preceding eighteen months on Constitution Street with a human rights framework. My written constitution seemed to be nearing completion but it needed some amendments. I realised that there was one important neighbour I had not yet interviewed.

Margaret is someone whom I pass every day and always nod to but had never had a full conversation with. I knew her name but she didn't know mine.

Lollipop lady Margaret has been crossing over Constitution Street for forty-three years. Every week day between 8am and 9am and 3pm and 4pm, she steps out into the middle of the busy road and stops the traffic so that pupils from Leith Primary School and their parents can safely cross. There is no room for hesitation or doubt in her job. Held aloft in her right hand, the lollipop stick looks like the sceptre belonging to Lady Justice. As first year primary school pupils are taught, she is a person who helps us. She shows us the way forward.

Well I'd like to think I'm respected, eh. Just like you try and respect other people I suppose.

Margaret was born two streets away and had her wedding reception in the Assembly Rooms on Constitution Street in 1965. *And if I mind right, we ate broth, steak pie and trifle. That was your choice in them days.* Her road safety patrol crossing, to use its official title, is in between the tower block and the park, at 161 Constitution Street.

It was a freezing cold day when we met. The low-lying haar combined with an icy North Sea wind and I had to keep my thumbs firmly tucked into clenched fists inside my coat pockets. I was also feeling strangely nervous about the interview. I think because I knew it would be the last of the sixty recorded conversations and the prevailing constitutional climate of a pre-Brexit fog made me feel under pressure to come to some conclusions.

As we stood chatting at 3pm, the school bell rang and a steady stream of children and families trickled across Constitution Street under Margaret's care. Everyone greeted her by name and she knew each of theirs.

At a Crossroads

I don't think the kids would have a clue what my surname is. It's always just Margaret. And again, half of them that I've taken over, I've take the mothers over too. I'll sometimes get a wee cuddle, which is quite nice, eh.

I can remember the lollipop lady from my school days in Dundee. Funnily enough, I think she was also called Margaret. The other thing I remember about Dundee Margaret is having one day seen her take off her tabard and hat at the end of a shift. I was both fascinated that she might lead a life beyond the uniform and slightly disappointed to have some of the neon-yellow magic dispelled.

Leith Margaret told me that when she first took up post in the 1970s her uniform was a source of fascination for visiting sailors strolling up and down Constitution Street from the docks. They apparently posed beside her for photographs. *Back when I was a bit more trim, mind!*

She has seen a lot of change on the street and surrounding area in the past four decades. The lollipop stick has twice been stolen while she lent it against the wall to talk to a passer-by. Most of all, while stood on this spot for four decades and across successive generations, the young people of Leith have put their trust in her at the start and close of every day. In agreeing for me to do a work experience stint with her, Margaret placed her trust in me.

It seems a very diverse mix of people?

Aye. Well Leith is very, very cosmopolitan. We've got all nationalities that go to Leith primary. And the kids are nice. The parents are nice. A lot of the parents can't talk English but they try their best and you always get a smile or a hello from them, you know.

The quiet, honest decency of ordinary folk like Margaret has been missing in our national constitutional debates. Margaret told me that no one had ever asked to interview her in forty-three years of the job. The people in real positions of leadership are those who help us day to day – lollipop ladies, teachers, nurses, police officers, parents and more. They have been as hidden in plain sight as the Burns statue on Constitution Street. They were here all along. We just don't always take the time to stop, look and listen.

Much of the apathy people have with party politics stems from people feeling unnoticed and underrepresented. Many votes in the referendums were a form of protest. People said that they didn't feel listened to. They no longer trusted the conventional way of doing politics.

I learnt a lot about trust and listening in the street interviews. People trusted me to record and share some of their own stories. I tried to be as mindful of how I found people as what I did with the evidence. This was my duty of care. Rather than following the linear structure of one house number after another, I started across the road with the neighbours I knew best and then asked each person I met for a further introduction. The meetings and flow of learning then extended outward like concentric, connecting ripples.

It was an immersive experience for me personally. Word soon spread locally that there was a woman with a notepad and a small, black dog asking lots of questions. The sense of daily recognition felt good on the whole. I, too, was listened to. It was grounding to have this sense of purpose and to have considerable community support. Sifting and analysing the evidence of human rights in practice taught me valuable lessons about attachment, about presence and absence, about what I want to keep and what I want to let go of. I want to retain the courage to send handwritten letters. And I want to make fewer assumptions about people.

The downside to the local visibility was a lack of privacy. There were times when I wanted to cross over the road to avoid someone. Or to step out of my front door and not immediately meet someone who knew my name and much of my own personal baggage. For example, there is a tributary to Constitution Street in between my flat and the Port O' Leith bar, Maritime Lane, where I always happened to be walking when I received bad personal news by phone. I slumped down onto the cobbles, wet with beer, piss and rain and wanted to be alone in my immediate and messy processing of difficulty. But I was never truly alone. Someone would inevitably see me and call out.

It was at times and places like this that it felt overly exposing and invasive to have my work and home lives so intertwined. On the brief visits to streets elsewhere in the world during 2017 and 2018, I enjoyed the momentary anonymity. However, the project that I crafted was about exploring a living constitution and so the fieldwork, both positive and negative, had to be lived as a daily, personal practice. I had to stand by my true expression of self, in the same way that I asked open and searching questions of others in the interviews.

To be fully constituted is to stand together with someone. Standing with my neighbours, I learnt as much about myself as about the common ground we walk upon. The process was about side by side conversations, much like the mix of the old and new, commercial and residential buildings of the street are sequential. I found that side-by-side dialogue is usually more cooperative and less combative than when facing each other directly. It allows for the possibility of travelling together in the same direction.

While drafting the Bill of Rights, my feet did the work of encounter, up and down, around and around. Conversation means to turn around on the spot. It is an exchange of experiences, a form of hospitality from one person to another – we select what to keep, what to share and what to give away, and in the physical act of turning and seeing, or hearing something new, conversation is like an improvised dance. I noticed that this dance of conversation was set to a different tempo depending on the time of day and season. By and large, the light and the weather dictated the unfolding of a moment and a mood. The long, dark winters in Scotland can make us inwardly contemplative. This makes us doubt ourselves and feel more anxious than we perhaps should.

I noticed too that my positive regard for the street and feeling safe and secure faded when the light did. Writing inside my flat on dark evenings, I was alone, save for the wordless, knowing company of a snoring hound. The nocturnal sounds outside and below the window – a can being kicked along the pavement, a fox tearing into a rubbish bag, someone vomiting on the steps, or the shout of football chants outside a bar – could be amplified to feel like something threatening. By contrast, the flow of daytime, domestic noises like birdsong, pushchair wheels, skateboarding, or a baby crying, seemed reassuringly routine and harmless. Perhaps it is because I belong more to one mood of the street than the other, or it is because I fear what I can't see in the dark and thus don't understand. Everything will feel better in the morning, my mum used to tell me when I was upset as a child. She is also fond of reminding me now that it will all be ok in the end and that if it's not, then it's not the end.

At the end of this exploration, I don't know for certain what the constitutional future of the UK has in store. I do think we will work it out though, because as Donald, the mechanic from no. 86, said at the start of this journey, we are still talking to one another. I've learnt more from conversations on Constitution Street than I ever did in a classroom or courtroom. I had previously worked in human rights outreach all over the world, in post-conflict zones such as Kosovo and Sierra Leone and in the fledgling democracy of post-apartheid South Africa. Only now do I know that the small contribution I have to make is here at home, on this spot, at the meeting place of the sea and the city at 55° North, -3° West and an altitude of eleven metres.

Paying attention to everyday change has helped me to keep pace with bigger changes in the wider world and in myself. Belonging on Constitution Street has been a rite of passage. Human rights really do belong in the small places closest to home. Bearing witness to this has been my personal protest against the rising tide of inequalities and political dysfunctionality. Much like the extraordinary people doing ordinary jobs, we don't always appreciate legal protections until we lose them. Human rights fulfilment is a lived experience of checks and balances.

Like all anxious people, I can be indecisive by nature but the lived experience on the street has helped me to settle on some reflections and hopes. Now is the moment for the UK to ask itself some soul-searching questions about the kind of country it wants to be. Brexit has laid bare deep social divisions and tested the union of constituent nations to the limit. Many neighbours told me that they no longer recognise Britishness in their identity. For me, a big problem with Brexit – British Exit – is that there is no longer such a place as Britain. The United Kingdom is nominally a four-nation state but England with 84% of the population and 82% of the electorial power in Westminster dominates discourse. When Scotland and Northern Ireland are exited from the EU against the will of their people, I believe that the pretence of a United Kingdom will be over. Going forward, England, Scotland, Ireland and Wales need to become equal, interdependent neighbours, side-by-side, with all the affection and respect for difference that can be nurtured in a neighbourhood of people. We need a new narrative. Lollipop lady Margaret put it best:

My grandchildren that stay here, their dad's English. They talk more English than what they do Scottish, eh. My granddaughter couldnae understand how I call people 'hen'. 'Why do you call people hen, granny?' I said, just like how down in England, they call them 'love', we call them 'hen'.

As with our words of affection, we have far more in common with our neighbours over the border than what separates us. I believe that now is the time to move away from flag-waving nationalism of any kind. Rather, we should nurture a place-based commons, street by street, to provide a way through the wreckage of nation-state politics. Local, active participation in clusters small enough that we see one another on a regular basis is where democracy – people power – can meaningfully flourish. These clusters could take the form of citizen assemblies made up of an intersectional mix of residents on rotation.[1] [2]

I still think that Scottish independence is the most pragmatic way to progress this democratic change. But it is just the beginning. The hard work begins after independence, when power should be further decentralised and devolved out of the capital city and into communities – communities roughly the size of a long street – and linked to other place-based communities across the world in the shared pursuit of a fair and dignified life. In this way, we will put our authority and trust in the people who have our best interests at heart, because they will be their own best interests too. People will be sovereign.

Step one on the road ahead is to draft a statement of collective expression and intent. The process of drafting this rights-based constitution will be as crucial as the resulting document. It must be fully inclusive of all walks of life. With human dignity at its core, negotiating and agreeing the constitution, street by street at scale, will give us back our sense of common purpose after a period of disorientating flux. It will be the compass to help navigate a path through the low-lying mist or haar. I believe this because I have experienced it in microcosm.

This rights-based approach requires participation, accountability, non-discrimination, equality and legality.[3] And we need not start from scratch. The Universal Declaration of Human Rights, and the human rights agreements that came after it, was written precisely for a moment like now. It provides the legal framework to connect the global and the local. Scotland would then be committing itself to 'take all necessary steps to use the maximum of available resources to progressively realise the rights of everyone.' This is the legal obligation undertaken by countries implementing economic, social and cultural rights, including rights to an adequate standard of living and to the highest available standard of physical and mental health, and would prioritise the rights of the most vulnerable in society.[4]

Our constitution should also be a living document, open to contemporary interpretation and new, unforeseen ways of knowing in its amendments. One of the things I value most in my neighbourhood is intergenerational friendships. A street community needs the wisdom and experience of its older residents like Margaret, balanced with the idealism and energy of the young, like my neighbour Maddie. On Constitution Street, my research focus was our lives together in the present day. I kept my timeframe as January 2017–June 2018, tracking the passing of the EU Withdrawal legislation through Parliament. However, people who have known the street much longer than I have indulged my interest in local history. To understand where we are now, and where we might be going in the future, I thought it was important to acknowledge where we have come from.

My hope is that when the street tarmac is dug open once again for the planned extension of the Edinburgh Trams route in 2020, I can put some of our present day stories into a time capsule for archaeologists, or future residents, to unearth. This date will coincide with the centenary of the Leith plebiscite to join with Edinburgh. In addition to the stories told in this book, I can include updates on how human rights have since been realised closest to home. For example, Maddie is now at secondary school and takes the number sixteen bus early each morning to journey across the city to her new school. I know that she is in safe hands because the driver of the bus was taught road safety by Margaret, our lollipop lady. He wound down the driver's window of the bus to say a friendly hello when I was stood with Margaret in the middle of the road.

Yeah. He's one of my bairns too.

And Merwe, Maddie's Afghan counterpart. She made it to Germany and was reunited with her family after four years apart. She phoned me from Athens airport as she boarded the plane. It happened to be 20 June 2018, World Refugee Day. She is now enrolled at school and is writing more of her own story:

Please include this also Jemma — I just want to tell other women or girls: You can do this. Never think that you can't do this. I kept trying my best and you should too.

The courage of young women like Maddie and Merwe inspires me to be braver. When I started out on the street-walk, I made a commitment to myself that I would invite everyone I interviewed to a meal at the end of my research, to thank them. The thought of hosting a big party and giving a welcome speech terrified me. I was anxious that no one would come. Or, the converse, that everyone invited would bring their partner, friend and dog and I wouldn't be able to feed them all. In the end, Fay and Niall from Nobles pub at no. 44A helped me to host a sit-down meal for sixty people. Politicians sat side by side with publicans. Neighbours who had never met one another shared supper and became friends. I gave a speech. People laughed and said nice things. My extended family turned up uninvited, and I was very grateful that they did. I felt a huge wave of catharsis wash over me. It felt like coming home. As Margaret said, *You know yourself, once you get up, have a cup of tea, get yourself ready, you're fine. Sometimes it's just the thought.*

Standing in the middle of the road, Margaret took my cold hands and warmed them inside hers. She has spent her whole life warming hands on Constitution Street.

Aye, I've never moved. And I wouldn't want to. You know, I'm quite happy here.

I've been quite happy here too, on the whole. I just didn't always realise that until I took the time to think about it and to see myself through my neighbours' eyes. However, unlike Margaret, I know that one day, in the not too distant future, I will need to move to another street. Bonnie is fading now and when she goes, I don't want to stay in our home by myself. I will be ready to begin a new chapter of my life and grow my family in other ways. But wherever I cross over to next, I will take a bit of Constitution Street with me.

Right darlings, over you go, thank you. That's us. See you tomorrow hen!
Margaret, Lollipop Lady, 161 Constitution Street

So with the darkest day behind
Our ship of hope will steer
And when in doubt just keep in mind
Our motto is persevere.

Inscription in stone, Water of Leith river path[1]

Epilogue

It's in between a dark night and a bright day. Inside my flat, I have been woken from a fitful sleep. I grasp for the alarm clock on the bedside table. 05:00 flashes in neon blue, the colour of facts and emergencies. It is a fact that the alarm is not set to ring until two hours later. I reach for the cold side of the pillow and bury myself back into the search for sleep. All the while, a small, black dog is relentlessly pawing at my shoulder and whimpering, whining. She yawns anxiously. A dog is always in the present moment. Her tummy makes a gurgling sound. Sleep is gone. I pull back the covers.

Together, we pad down the stone steps of the tenement stairs at increasing speed. I push open the cracked front door onto the dawn street-scene outside. There is near silence. The pubs are shut. There are no cars on the road. It is late June and the seagulls are up above, guarding their rooftop nests. A faulty street light flickers like a half-smile and a fat moon is tucked behind shifting clouds. I can feel but not yet see a fox watching us.

Beyond, there is the sea and the wider world, a world full of more streets, avenues, terraces, lanes, wynds, boulevards and places stretched out on and on and on. Constitution Road in Dundee. Constitution Hill in Johannesburg. Constitution Avenue in Washington DC.

Near the end of my road, at the start of this day, in the middle of this year, I crouch down low and hold my nose in a gagging reflex. I take a black, plastic bag from a pyjama pocket and mop at a pool of steaming, liquid dog shite. So this is how the day starts. There is a dog with a dodgy constitution and me in pyjamas and a pink, knitted hat. It is unremarkable and entirely with precedent.

In a moment, the summer sun will begin to rise above the tenements. It will bathe us with the bright light of a new day. Sirius, The Dog Star, and the closest star in the night's sky, will rise at the same time as the sun. We will have just passed the longest day of the year in the Northern Hemisphere so there will be lots to see, to hear, to do and to feel.

In a moment, back inside my flat at the start of my day, I will reach for my phone. Following, scrolling, liking, clicking, searching, charging, inside my palm, the one-dimensional, digital surface will glow hot and angry with news from the wider world.

The European Union (Withdrawal) Act will receive royal assent. The UK Cabinet will be in meltdown with the prospect of a no-deal Brexit. EU citizens living in the UK will be instructed to pay for registration papers. President Trump will play golf in Scotland, the country of his immigrant mother. The England football team will nearly bring home the World Cup. Support for Scottish independence will fluctuate. The value of the pound will fall. There will be stockpiling of medicines and food. A rescue ship containing 400 frightened people will be refused entry into a European port. Along the US-Mexican border, children will be separated from their parents and imprisoned in cages. It will be the hottest summer in a lifetime. All across the land, people will be sweating and burning up with sticky anxiety. There will be constitutional crisis in the times of our lives. The country will have gone to the dogs. It will be a wake-up call.

Also in a moment, I will look out the window and onto the street. A wisp of cigarette smoke will rise from beside a towelled figure sitting on her doorstep. Someone has been up all night worrying about her daughters. In a moment, porridge will be thickened and stirred, a kettle hiss and a school uniform will be scraped from the floor. Someone is cared for. In a moment, steel shutters will be heaved upward, chairs stacked, broken glass swept and doors unlocked. Someone is opening up. In a moment, future lovers will nod a shy hello then look away. Someone is imagining. In a moment, a prayer mat will be rolled out and kneeled upon. Someone still has faith. In a moment, the wheels of a pull-along suitcase will be dragged across pavement slabs, sounding like the tide raking across pebbles on a shore. Someone is lingering in Leith. In a moment, I will call out the window 'Mind how you go.' Someone nearly stepped in dog shite. In a moment, a number sixteen bus will round the corner past the Buddhist temple, Pierinos chippie, the Rabbie Burns statue, the Port O' Leith bar and onto Constitution Street. Someone will shout 'Wait!' And we do, we do keep waiting and minding. And all the rest. Biding ourselves ready for change. Because this is our moment. We are coming up in the world.

Wherever you are in the world, take up the habit of a daily constitutional. Allow yourself to be surprised. The feeling of being listened to is almost indistinguishable from the feeling of being loved. And take care. In doing so, I think that, like me, you will begin to feel a bit more hopeful about the time of our lives.

I know that in this moment, while talking and listening with you, as though we are neighbours, that we will be alright on Constitution Street. Someone is going to write it all down, letter by letter. There will be laws and principles and even poetry. It will be guided by the stories of our past but not weighed down by them. It will recognise our interdependence and welcome all different types of people from other small places closest to home. It will be a living document, with time ahead for amendments. It will be called a Constitution. And we will hold it in our hands.

Jemma Neville,
Constitution Street,
26 June 2018

Glossary

ain: own

aye: yes

bairn: child

bard: poet

bonnie: good, pretty

breeches: short trousers

cairn: a mound of rough stones built as a memorial or landmark

chapping: knocking

clapshot: mix of mashed potato and turnip

close: alleyway

clype: to inform on someone

cooper: a maker of barrels

dreich: wet

fare: food

greetin: crying

ken: know

kith and kin: relatives

haar: sea fog

hamely: homely

hen: woman

hings: hangs

kirk: church

masel: myself

mibbe: maybe

mind: remember

neep: turnip

plaid: tartan cloth

popper: a recreational drug that makes a popping sound

scree: loose stones on a hill

smirry: light rain

stoop: a small raised platform or the entrance to a building

stoor: dust

tattie: potato

thro': through

wee: small

windae: window

woose: wuss, weak or lacking in confidence

wynd: a narrow lane

Endnotes

Welcome

1. R (Miller) v Secretary of State for Exiting the European Union [2017] UKSC 5.
2. The European Union (Withdrawal) Act 2018, Hansard, vol.792.
3. A note on Brexit and sources of human rights law: The European Convention on Human Rights (ECHR) and its accompanying Protocols will continue in effect, regardless of the UK's memb ership status in the European Union as it is a regional instrument of the Council of Europe not the EU. The Council of Europe includes countries outside of the EU, such as Russia, Turkey and Ukraine. Obligations under United Nations treaty bodies will be unaffected by Brexit. However, protections through the EU Charter of Fundamental Rights and the European Social Charter will be lost if the UK leaves the EU.
4. The commons is a way of negotiating shared space and resources. This is explored further in the later chapter on the Right to Self-Determination.
5. Referred to as 'the social cure', the feeling that you share a social identity with others is reported to lead to multiple positive health outcomes. (Jetten, Jolanda (Ed.), Haslam, Catherine (Ed.), Haslam, Alexander S (Ed.). *The Social Cure: Identity, Health and Well-Being.* Psychology Press, 2012). Another form of recognition is being greeted by others in your group who you don't know. Like recognition between acquaintances, this has an ontological component such that they're signalling that they recognise you as a member of the group and that you belong. See examples from mass participation events, such as religious festivals or football matches (Neville, Fergus Gilmour, Reicher, Stephen David. "The experience of collective participation: Shared identity, relatedness and emotionality." *Contemporary Social Science*, 6(3), 2011, pp. 377-396).

Setting Out on a Constitutional

1. The Scottish Human Rights Commission is the national human rights institution for Scotland. Established by The Scottish Commission for Human Rights Act 2006, the Commission is a Category A national human rights institution, meaning that it can report directly to the United Nations Human Rights Council.

2. The Scotland Act 1998, Schedule 5.

3. The Changin' Scotland Festival in March 2015 was organised by Gerry Hassan, Jean Urquhart, Mairi McFadyen and Andy Summers.

4. Human rights law has been developed through common law arguments in addition to use of legislation such as The Human Rights Act. See Lord Bingham on the rule of law: 'All persons and authorities within the state, whether public or private, should be bound by and entitled to the benefit of laws publicly and prospectively promulgated and publicly administered in the courts… the law must afford adequate protection of fundamental Human Rights.' From a lecture by Rt. Hon Lord Bingham of Cornhill KG. "The Rule of Law." House of Lords, London. 16 November 2006. The full transcript can be found on the Centre for Public Law, University of Cambridge website.

5. Agreement between the United Kingdom Government and the Scottish Government on a referendum on independence for Scotland, Edinburgh, 15 October 2012.

6. R (Miller) v Secretary of State for Exiting the European Union [2017] UKSC 5.

7. The Sewel Convention applies when the UK Parliament wants to legislate on a matter within the devolved competence of the Scottish Parliament, National Assembly for Wales or Northern Ireland Assembly. Under the terms of the Convention, the UK Parliament will not normally do so without the relevant devolved institution having passed a legislative consent motion.

8. On the accountability gap, see "Models of Incorporation and Justiciability of Economic, Social and Cultural Rights", a report authored by Dr Katie Boyle for the Scottish Human Rights Commission, November 2018, p. 6.

9. For more discussion on constitutional theory, see the inaugural lecture of Professor Jeff King, University College London, "The Democratic Case for a Written Constitution," April 2018. See also arguments from A.C. Grayling on the merits of a codified constitution for the UK, in a lecture on behalf of the Foundation for Law, Justice and Society at Oxford University.

10. In its 'White Paper on Scottish Independence' ahead of the 2014 referendum, the Scottish Government stated that an independent Scotland would have a written constitution and that the Scottish Parliament would convene an independent constitutional convention to debate and draft the constitution. Noting that 'a constitution is the basis of everyday life, not separate from it', the process to shape the constitution was intended to be fully participatory. However, there was little detail provided on

how an inclusive process would be ensured and of the role of civil society. See *Scotland's Future: Your Guide to an Independent Scotland*, the Scottish Government, November 2013, pp.351–353.

11. The Universal Declaration of Human Rights, Adopted and Proclaimed by General Assembly resolution 217 A (III), 10 December 1948.

12. Klug, Francesca. "The Universal Declaration of Human Rights at Seventy: Rejuvenate or Retire?" *The Political Quarterly*, April 2019, p. 6.

13. The Universal Declaration of Human Rights, together with The International Covenant on Civil and Political Rights (ICCPR, 1966) with its two Optional Protocols and The International Covenant on Economic, Social and Cultural Rights (ICESCR, 1966), are known collectively as The International Bill of Rights. All international instruments are monitored by the United Nations. Countries that have signed and ratified the agreements have to submit regular reports to show how they are implementing the rights in the treaty. The reports are examined by a committee of experts, which publishes concerns and recommendations. Many instruments that came after the UDHR were intended to rectify omissions, for example on disability, sexual orientation and age, that reflected the context and time within which the UDHR was drafted.

14. The Human Rights Act 1998, Schedule 1.

15. The Scotland Act 1998, s. 29(2)(d) and The Human Rights Act, s. 4. If Scottish Ministers do not adhere to the Convention, legislation may be struck down by Scottish courts or may result in a ruling from The European Court of Human Rights in Strasbourg. This is different to the UK Parliament and the strict doctrine of parliamentary supremacy.

16. The Scotland Act 1998, Schedule 5, s. 7.

17. There is precedent from elsewhere in the world for devolved nations and regions introducing more robust human rights mechanisms than at the sovereign state level. In Switzerland, some cantons have greater human rights protections than at confederal level, and in Argentina both federal and devolved governments have directly incorporated international human rights treaties into constitutions. For an overview of comparative examples, see *Models of Incorporation and Justiciability for Economic Social and Cultural Rights*, a report authored by Dr. Katie Boyle for the Scottish Human Rights Commission, November 2018, pp.14–17.

18. See Klug, Francesca. "The Universal Declaration of Human Rights at Seventy: Rejuvenate or Retire?" *The Political Quarterly*, April 2019.

19. As affirmed by the Vienna Declaration and Programme of Action, adopted by the World Conference on Human Rights in Vienna on 25 June 1993.

20. Shepherd, Nan. *The Living Mountain*. Canongate, 2011.

The Lay of the Land

1. For an overview of wildlife found along the river, see the work of The Water of Leith Conservation Trust.
2. The drinking fountain was named "Le Cinque Lampade" by the Italian diaspora.
3. Leith Burgh Records, ref SL224.
4. Harris, Stuart. *The Place Names of Edinburgh: Their Origins and History*. Gordon Wright Publishing Ltd, 1996.
5. "Williamson's directory for the City of Edinburgh, Canongate, Leith and suburbs," July 1793–July 1794. digital.nls.uk/83084176.
6. The Constitution of the United States of America, ratified 21 June 1788.
7. The United States Declaration of Independence, ratified 4 July 1776.
8. The Declaration of the Rights of Man and of the Citizen, adopted 26 August 1789.
9. Members of the Scottish diaspora including exiled radicals and intellectuals like Thomas Paine were influential in the drafting of the US Constitution.

The Right to Life

1. An exhibition and accompanying book, *Past Lives of Leith*, by Julie Franklin, Carmelita Troy, Kate Britton, Donald Wilson and John A Lawson will be available through Museums and Galleries Edinburgh in 2019 with the exhibition running until the end of October 2019. Headland Archaeology undertook the archaeological dig in summer 2009, with analysis by the City of Edinburgh Council Archaeology Service, in partnership with the universities of Aberdeen and Dundee.
2. The Declaration of Arbroath is a declaration of Scottish independence, made in 1320. It is in the form of a letter in Latin submitted to Pope John XXII, dated 6 April 1320, intended to confirm Scotland's status as an independent, sovereign state and defending Scotland's right to use military action when unjustly attacked.
3. Marshall, James Scott. *The Life and Times of Leith*. John Donald Publishers Ltd., 1986, p. 68.
4. Salinger, J.D. *The Catcher in the Rye*. Penguin Books, 1945.
5. Burns, Robert. "Comin' Thro' The Rye". Verse 4.
6. MacDiarmid, Hugh. "The Caledonian Antisyzygy and the Gaelic Idea." *The Modern Scot*. July 1931.
7. The Universal Declaration of Human Rights, Article 1: "All human beings are born free and equal in dignity and rights. There are endowed with reason and conscience and should act towards one another in a spirit of brotherhood."

The Right to Education

1. The Immigration Act 2016, s. 67, placed a requirement on the Secretary of State to 'make arrangements to relocate to the United Kingdom and support a specified number of unaccompanied refugee children from other countries in Europe.'
2. "Children needing asylum in UK not being helped by Dubs scheme", The Guardian, 23 October 2017.
3. Sappho,. Barnstone, Willis. (Translation.) *The Complete Poems of Sappho*. Shambhala Publications, 2009, p. 26.
4. UNHCR Greece Factsheet, July 2018, and UNICEF Press Release, Refugee and migrant children arriving on Greek islands up by one-third in 2018, September 2018.

The Right to Housing

1. I like to think that pet dogs have been appreciated on Constitution Street far back in time as, next to the butchered bones of farm animals, archaeologists found the unfractured skeleton of a collie-sized dog buried next to human remains dating from the seventeenth century. This location at no. 102 Constitution Street is now a restaurant called *The Chop House*. Source: White, R. and O'Connell, C. Excavations on the Site of Balmerino House, Constitution Street, Leith. SAIR 41, 2009.
2. Edinburgh 2050 City Vision, see www.edinburgh2050.com.
3. Rae, Alasdair. "Analysis of Short-Term Lets Data for Edinburgh." A briefing note commissioned for the Scottish Green Party, 1 November 2017.
4. Stevenson, Robert Louis. *Kidnapped*. Cassell and Company Ltd, 1886.
5. "Edinburgh by Numbers 2018" by Edinburgh City Council.
6. Hansard vol. 462 cc2121–231, Minister of Health Mr Aneurin Bevan on the passing of The Housing Act 1949.
7. The Homelessness etc. (Scotland) Act 2003 removed the test of whether someone has a priority need for housing (the test is still in operation across England and Wales, restricting many people's right to support). See "Housing is a human right," a report by Shelter Scotland, January 2019.
8. In 2017-2018, official statistics record 3,200 incidences where local authorities failed to provide homeless households with accommodation. See "Shelter Scotland Impact Report, 2017/18".
9. In 2017-2018 in Scotland, there were 400 placements of households with children or pregnant women in temporary accommodation for more than the maximum seven days stipulated in law. 280 of these breaches occurred in Edinburgh. In December 2017, an amendment to the Unsuitable Accommodation Order came into force

which reduced the amount of time that families are able to spend in temporary accommodation deemed to be unsuitable. See "Housing is a human right," a report by Shelter Scotland, January 2019.

10. Report of the United Nations Special Rapporteur on adequate housing as a component of the right to an adequate standard of living, and on the right to non-discrimination in this context, presented to the United Nations Human Rights Council, December 2013. See also the later "Statement on Visit to the United Kingdom, by Professor Philip Alston, United Nations Special Rapporteur on extreme poverty and human rights", 16 November 2018.

11. CESCR General Comment No. 4: The Right to Adequate Housing (Art. 11 (1) of the International Covenant on Economic Social and Cultural Rights, para. 7). Adopted at the Sixth Session of the Committee on Economic, Social and Cultural Rights, on 13 December 1991 (Contained in Document e/1992/23).

12. "Meet the most dangerous wee woman in the world (that America has never heard of)", Piers Morgan for the Mail Online, 20 April 2015.

13. "Man kept four-foot alligator in bath at his tower-block flat," The Scotsman, 23 December 2004.

14. Dunbar, R. I. M. "Neocortex size as a constraint on group size in primates." *Journal of Human Evolution*. vol. 22, no. 6, June 1992, pp. 469–493.

15. Lang, Olivia. *The Lonely City*. Canongate, 2017.

16. Arendt, Hannah. *The Origins of Totalitarianism*. Schocken Books, 1951.

17. "The International Covenant on Economic, Social and Cultural Rights", Article 11.

18. The Constitution of the Republic of South Africa, Article 26: (1) Everyone has the right to have access to adequate housing; (2) The state must take reasonable legislative and other measures, within its available resources, to achieve the progressive realisation of this right; (3) No one may be evicted from their home, or have their home demolished, without an order of court made after considering all the relevant circumstances. No legislation may permit arbitrary evictions.

19. Government of the Republic of S. Afr. v. Grootboom, [2000] ZACC 19; 2001 (1) SA 46; 2000 (11) BCLR 1169 (S. Afr.).

20. For a discussion of the case, see *The Strange Alchemy of Life and Law* by Albie Sachs, Oxford University Press, 2009, chapter 7, "The Judge Who Cried: The Judicial Enforcement of Socio-Economic Rights", p. 191.

21. Scottish Government Poverty Statistics (published 28 March 2019): 20% of people in Scotland (and 24% of children) were living in relative poverty after housing costs in 2015–2018. NHS Lothian (Edinburgh Health and Social Care Partnership Joint Strategic Needs Assessment Locality Overview) puts poverty in the Leith electoral ward at 27%, or 957 children.

22. Constitution Street spans several zones in the Scottish Index of Multiple Deprivation (SIMD) postcode map. Postcodes are ranked in deciles 1–10 across Scotland for

different quality of life indicators, 1 being most deprived and 10 the least. Overall, Constitution Street ranks 4, just below the national mean for levels of deprivation. However, the housing domain rank is the lowest at 1 (in the top 5% most deprived in Scotland) and there is a wide range of values for education/skills, health and rates of crime. This demonstrates the socio-economic diversity of the street's residents.

23. United Nations, "2018 Revision of World Urbanization Prospects".

The Right to Food

1. The right to food has been broken down by the Committee on Economic, Social and Cultural Rights body into different elements, namely food must be available, accessible (economically and physically), adequate (satisfying dietary needs, safe and culturally acceptable) and sustainable: General Comment No 12 on the right to adequate food, UN Doc E/C. 12/1999/5, 12 May 1999.

2. Between 1st April 2017 and 31st March 2018, The Trussell Trust's foodbank network distributed 170,625 three-day emergency food supplies to people in crisis in Scotland, a 17% increase on the previous year. The top reasons for referral to a food bank were 'low income', 'benefit delay', 'benefit change' and 'debt', suggesting a causal link between the implementation of social security and the food insecurity.

3. See the responses to the Scottish Government's "A Connected Scotland: our strategy for tackling social isolation and loneliness and building stronger social connections", 18 December 2018.

4. *Book of Occurrences in the Life of Captain James Smith of Edinburgh* (1801 - 1878), copyright Isobel Barr Neville, p. 82.

5. "The Slave's Lament", lyrics by Robert Burns, first published in 1792 in vol. 4 of the *Scots Musical Museum*.

6. The UK imports about 30% (by value) of all its food from other EU Member States. Source: UK Government Department for Environment Food and Rural Affairs, "Food Statistics in your pockets 2017 - Global and UK supply." 2017, www.gov.uk/government/publications/food-statistics-pocketbook-2017/food-statistics-in-your-pocket-2017-global-and-uk-supply. For a discussion on Brexit and food security, see the work of the University of Edinburgh's Global Academy of Agriculture and Food Security.

The Right to Health

1. In the most affluent areas of Scotland, men experience 23.8 more years of good health and women experience 22.6 more years compared to the most deprived areas.

NHS Scotland, "What are health inequalities?", www.healthscotland.scot/health-in-equalities/what-are-health-inequalities [accessed 17 June 2019].

2. National Records for Scotland. "Alcohol specific deaths in Scotland, 2000 onwards". 2018, www.nrscotland.gov.uk/statistics-and-data/statistics/statistics-by-theme/vital-events/deaths/alcohol-deaths/alcohol-specific-deaths-new-definition [accessed 17 June 2019]

3. Scotch Whisky Association and others v The Lord Advocate and another [2017] UKSC 76.

4. Scottish Government, "The Scottish Health Survey", 2017.

5. "Sunshine in Leith" is a song by The Proclaimers, released in August 1988. It has been adopted as an anthem by Hibernian Football Club supporters and was a stage musical (2007) and then film (2013) of the same name.

6. When Thomas Jefferson asserted the inalienable rights of life, liberty, and the pursuit of happiness in the United States Declaration of Independence 1776, he was said to have been influenced by the writings of Henry Home, Lord Kames. Kames was a Scottish lawyer and moral philosopher who argued for the right to 'the pursuit of happiness' in his *Essays on the Principles of Morality and Natural Religion,* 1779.

7. "Symphony No. 2: The Age of Anxiety" by Leonard Bernstein, 1949, is a piece for piano and orchestra.

8. The Constitution of The World Health Organisation, 1946, states that 'health is a state of complete physical, mental and social well-being and not merely the absence of disease or infirmity.'

The Right to Freedom of Religious Belief

1. Marshall, James. *The Life and Times of Leith.* John Donald Publishers Ltd, 1986, p. 65.

2. *Father Ted* was a British-made sitcom produced by Hat Trick Productions for Channel 4. It featured three priests who shared a house on a fictional island set off Ireland's west coast. The series ran from 1995 - 1998. Mrs Doyle was the housekeeper in the priests' house.

3. At the Conservative Party conference in Birmingham, 5 October 2016, Prime Minister Theresa May said in a speech: "if you believe you're a citizen of the world, you're a citizen of nowhere. You don't understand what the very word 'citizenship' means." The speech pitted 'international elites' against 'the people down the road.'

4. 'Choose life' is the beginning of a stream of consciousness by character Mark Renton in the film *Trainspotting*, 1996, directed by Danny Boyle, written by John Hodge, and based on the novel by Irvine Welsh.

5. In 1992 James Joyce told fellow writer Arthur Powell: 'For myself, I always write about Dublin, because if I can get to the heart of Dublin I can get to the heart of all

the cities of the world. In the particular is contained the universal.' Joyce argued that universal experiences were to be found, not with gods or heroes, but in mundane urban lives. A reference to 'A Shout in the Street' comes from Chapter 2 of *Ulysses* by James Joyce, Shakespeare and Company, 1922. "Stephen jerked his thumb towards the window, saying: 'That is God…' 'What?' Mr Deasy asked. 'A shout in the street,' Stephen answered, shrugging his shoulders."

The Right to Work

1. Analysis of youth (age 16-24) unemployment, excluding those in full-time education, for Scotland as a whole. The data analysed is based on the Labour Force Survey, produced quarterly for The Office of National Statistics (UK).
2. *Jude* is a 1996 British period drama film directed by Michael Winterbottom, and written by Hossein Amini, based on Thomas Hardy's novel *Jude the Obscure*.
3. Marshall, James Scott. *The Life and Times of Leith*. John Donald Publishers Ltd, 1986, p. 45.
4. *How To Change the World*, a film written and directed by Jerry Rothwell, 2015.
5. Muir, John. *My First Summer in the Sierra*. Houghton Mufflin, 1911.
6. Scottish Government, "Growth Sector Statistics Database". October 2017.
7. *Williamson's Directory for the City of Edinburgh, Canongate, Leith and suburbs, July 1793-July 1794*, available in the National Library of Scotland.
8. Jennings, Gemma. "The ecology of an urban colony of common terns Sterna hirundo in Leith Docks, Scotland." PhD thesis, University of Glasgow, 2012.
9. The Universal Declaration of Human Rights, Article 23 (2), (3).

The Right to Freedom of Expression

1. 'The Constructed Space' is a poem by W. S. Graham, in *New Collected Poems*, edited by Mathew Francis. Faber, 2004.
2. The United Nations International Criminal Tribunal for the Former Yugoslavia Outreach Programme.
3. Hutton, James. *Theory of the Earth*. Royal Society of Edinburgh, 1788.
4. Fergusson, Robert. 'Leith Races'. First published in *The Weekly Magazine*, 22 July 1773.
5. *Seagulls*, a play by Volcano Theatre, performed at The Leith Volcano, 119 Constitution Street, August 2017.

The Right to Private and Family Life

1. Burns wrote the lines as a prologue to be spoken by the actress Louise Fontenelle, 26 November 1792.
2. There was reportedly a spike in hate-crimes in the UK after the EU referendum. See Devine, Daniel, "The UK Referendum on Membership of the European Union as a Trigger Event for Hate Crimes", University of Southampton, 5 February 2018.
3. The Human Rights Act 1998, s. 4.
4. Should the UK later repeal The Human Rights Act, this would remove the direct incorporation of ECHR rights in domestic law but claimants could still take cases to Strasbourg (a lengthy and expensive process) and the domestic legal system have regard to Strasbourg jurisprudence. Effectively, we would be back to pre-1998. Lawyers may still try to develop human rights through law case law, arguing that human rights are now part of the common law in the UK. However, a repeal of The Human Rights Act would also require amendments to The Scotland Act 1998 with its human rights protections. This would be very unsettling for devolution arrangements and so may be politically unpalatable.
5. Data from The UK Electoral Commission.

The Right to Justice

1. Woolf, Virginia. *The Death of the Moth and Other essays*. The Hogarth Press, 1942.
2. *Book of Occurrences in the Life of Captain James Smith of Edinburgh* (1801-1878), copyright Isobel Barr Neville, pp. 27-31.
3. The Scotland Act 1998, s. 29 (2) and s. 57(2).
4. See Robert Napier v The Scottish Ministers (2005) SC 229.

The Right to the Environment

1. Carson, Rachel. *Silent Spring*. Houghton Mifflin, 1962, p. 215.
2. The Community Empowerment (Scotland) Act 2015 requiring local authorities to increase allotment provision and to develop food growing strategies is an example of where a rights based approach has been taken in law and policy to support access to food. For a more in-depth consideration of the commons as a new narrative in politics, see *Out of the Wreckage: A new politics for an age of crisis* by George Monbiot, Verso, 2017.
3. 'Think global, act local' is a phrase attributed to Scots town planner and social activist Patrick Geddes. See *Cities in Evolution: an introduction to town planning and to the study*

of civics, by Patrick Geddes, Williams and Norgate, 1915.

4. The Constitution of the Republic of Costa Rica, 1948, Article 50: 'Every person has the right to a healthy and ecologically balanced environment, being therefore entitled to denounce any acts that may infringe said right and claim redress for the damage caused.'

5. The Constitution of the Federative Republic of Brazil, 1988, Article 225: 'Everyone has the right to an ecologically balanced environment, which is a public good for the people's use and is essential for a healthy life. The Government and the community have a duty to defend and to preserve the environment for present and future generations.'

6. The Constitution of Colombia, 1991, Article 49: 'Public health and environmental protection are public services for which the State is responsible.'

7. The Charter of the Environment 2004, in force 2005.

8. The International Convention on Economic, Social and Cultural Rights, Article 12(1), (2(b)).

9. An example of this momentum, compared with other parts of the UK, is the Fairer Scotland Duty. In force from April 2018 as part of the Equality Act 2010, the duty requires public sector bodies to consider how to reduce socio-economic disadvantage when making strategic decisions. More information is available from the regulator of the duty, the Equality and Human Rights Commission.

10. See the report of the First Minister's Advisory Group on Human Rights Leadership: 'Recommendations for a new human rights framework to improve people's lives', December 2018; and 'Models of Incorporation and Justiciability for Economic, Social and Cultural Rights', a report authored by Dr Katie Boyle for the Scottish Human Rights Commission, November 2018.

11. The Housing Rights in Practice Project was a pilot as part of Scotland's National Action Plan on Human Rights. It was supported by the Scottish Human Rights Commission and delivered in partnership with the Edinburgh Tenants Federation and the Participation and Practice of Rights Project (PPR) based in Belfast.

12. On human dignity as a social minimum, see *Models of Incorporation and Justiciability for Economic, Social and Cultural Rights*, authored by Dr Katie Boyle for the Scottish Human Rights Commission, 2018, p. 8.

13. The European Convention on Human Rights, Article 13: 'The right to an effective remedy' requires all domestic remedies to have been exhausted before a case can be taken to Strasbourg.

14. López Ostra v Spain, Application No. 16798/90, A/303-C, [1994] ECHR 46, (1995) 20 EHRR 277, IHRL 3079 (ECHR 1994), 9 December 1994, European Court of Human Rights [ECHR].

15. Öneryildiz v. Turkey, Application No. 48939/99; (2005) 41 EHRR 20; [2004] ECHR 657; 18 BHRC 145, (2005); [2004] Inquest LR 108.

16. A Proposal for a new constitution for the Republic of Iceland, Articles 33, 34 and 35: 'the Nature and environment of Iceland'. For an overview of the participation process in Iceland to draft a new constitution, see the documentary *Blueberry Soup: How Iceland changed the way we think about democracy*, a film by Wilma's Wish Productions, directed by Eileen Jerrett, 2013.

17. The Constitution of the Republic of Ecuador 2008, Preamble: 'We women and men, the sovereign people of Ecuador... Hereby decide to build a new form of public coexistence, in diversity and in harmony with nature, to achieve the good way of living...'

18. Community Empowerment (Scotland) Act 2015.

19. Andy Wightman MSP has estimated that half of the privately-owned rural land is in the hands of 432 people (Andy Wightman, *The Poor Had No Lawyers*, Birlinn, 2010). This has been described by Tom Devine as 'the most concentrated pattern of land ownership in Europe' (Tom Devine, *The Scottish Nation: 1700–2000*, Penguin, 1999 p. 457).

20. The Land Reform (Scotland) Act 2016 makes explicit reference to the United Nations International Covenant on Economic, Social and Cultural Rights (ICESCR) as the guiding framework behind land reform in Scotland. The Act also strengthens community rights to buy and created obligations to consult communities in land reform processes. In the passage of the new land reform legislation through The Scottish Parliament, concerns over rights to housing, health, food, work and cultural life were debated as justifications for infringement of the right to private property. The human rights focus shifted from avoiding human rights violations to actively pursuing the progressive realisation of rights. See 'Human Rights and the Work of the Scottish Land Commission: a discussion paper' by Dr Kirsteen Shields, May 2018.

21. See the "United Kingdom – air pollution country fact sheet 2018," produced by the European Environment Agency.

The Right to Self-Determination

1. The Barcelona En Comú party was elected by a citizen-led platform opposing housing evictions. For an overview of Ada Calau's journey from housing rights activism to winning the mayoral contest, see the documentary film *Ada for Mayer*, directed by Pau Faus, 2016. Since 2014 more than 100 municipalities across Spain have approved motions to levy fines on banks with empty homes.

2. For thinking about the non-state to state model of democratic confederalism, based on learning from Rojava in northern Syria, see the writing of imprisoned leader Abdullah Öcalan.

3. *Autumn Journal* is the name of the Louis MacNeice long-form poem about anxiety, written in 1938 at the height of the civil war while travelling through Spain, published by Faber and Faber Ltd, 1939.
4. Scottish Government, 'Scotland's population needs a migration policy: discussion paper'. February 2018.

At a Crossroads

1. See the Governance and Community Engagement work led by Oliver Escobar, University of Edinburgh, and What Works Scotland.
2. For further consideration of citizen assemblies and constitutions, see the example of citizen assemblies formed in the Republic of Ireland in 2016, to debate repeal of the 8th constitutional amendment ahead of a national referendum in May 2018.
3. Known as the PANEL principles, a human rights-based approach is about making sure that people's rights are put at the centre of policies and practices.
4. This is the principle of progressive realisation. See the Committee on Economic, Social and Cultural Rights, General Comment No.3: The Nature of States Parties' Obligations (Art. 2, Para. 1, of the Covenant).

Epilogue

1. From one of five carved stones on the Water of Leith footpath at The Shore. The verse was reportedly written by a Leith Athletic football fan when the club returned to play football after the Second World War. It was chosen as an inscription for the pathway by my neighbour Iain Dick.

Acknowledgements

First and foremost, thank you to the people who appear in these pages. For personal safety reasons, some of the addresses have been changed, one name was changed and other names left out. Thanks also to those neighbours who shared stories that, for a variety of reasons, don't appear in the book. To those neighbours I have yet to meet, I hope you also recognise something of our street in my words. Thanks to Louise for first opening the door to me.

I acknowledge those who gave me their professional expertise including lawyer Katrin Oddsdóttir, archaeologist John Lawson, PC Mark Muir, Forth Ports Asset Manager Ray Clark, art therapist Simon Marshall, Dr Rowena Neville, Councillor Gordon Munro, Ben Macpherson MSP, architect Sam Moran, local history enthusiasts Iain Dick, Irene Reynolds and the staff at Edinburgh and Leith libraries. Any factual errors are mine alone.

Thank you to the Institute for Advanced Studies in Humanities, University of Edinburgh, for awarding me a Community Fellowship to undertake research in 2017 and to my roommate, Dr Sarah Brazil, for sharing our attic garret in the aptly named Hope Park Square. I appreciate the support of my colleagues at Voluntary Arts in trusting me to return to work after a sabbatical.

Thanks to the editors of *The Island Review* and *Bella Caledonia*, where some of the book's themes were first developed.

Thanks to Jim Flowers for keeping time. And Mel Esquerre for the breakfasts.

Annie Blaber, John Dargie and Scottish PEN gifted me space at Lesser Wearie bothy. Much of the editing of a book about a noisy street was completed in a tranquil Highland glen.

I am very grateful to my agent Jenny Brown, editor Jo Dingley and publishers Heather McDaid and Laura Jones at 404 Ink for believing in this book and allowing me to work with creative talent from my street – Morven Jones, Rob Smith and Jill Boulaxai – on the illustration, photography and cover artwork.

Thank you Dr Jacqui Kinghan, Faith Liddell, Claire Newton, Chitra Ramaswamy and Elizabeth Reeder for being wise, generous counsel and for commenting on drafts.

Love to my family – Ron, Tricia, Fergus and Lucy – for supporting me throughout the writing, and the not-writing, of this book. And to Isobel Neville for passing on an appreciation of letter-writing, public libraries and walking in Edinburgh.

Love to Zak Hanif for returning my letter and having been right up my street all along.

And finally thank you to Bonnie, my street-dog from Leith, without whom I wouldn't have had cause to walk up and down Constitution Street every day with such reverie. She's looking out of the window now with her paw raised, so it must be time to go.

Photo: Rob Smith

Jemma Neville has a background in human rights law and arts development. Originally from Dundee, she is now at home on Constitution Street, Leith, a place in between the city and the sea.

This is her first book.